Walking My Father's Fields:

Love Letters from a Daughter of the Land

By

Vernie Lynn Johnson DeMille

With illustrations by Jeremiah Moore

www.jeremiahmooreart.com

www.verniedemille.com

For Mom and Dad

Thank you for my life and my name,

for the love that fills my heart and the faith that fills my soul,
for memories that are precious

and dreams that are priceless.

It is my fondest wish that someday I will grow up

to be just like you.

Acknowledgments

I would like to thank the many people who helped me to accomplish this work and without whom it surely would not have made it to publication.

The entire Johnson clan, for being fodder for my thoughts and friends for my days and years. May God grant us many more years to laugh and love together.

Deena Ortiz, for wading her way through the comma spiced, over punctuated mess that I handed her to edit. You are an example of patience and kindness that I'm positive is unequaled in the literary world.

Marnie Gasik, for convincing a 9 year old that the thoughts in her head were worth writing down, for being an inspiring teacher, and for encouraging a life-long love of reading.

Lynn and Symbria Patterson, for being amazing friends and great farmers. I'd like to think that somewhere in Paradise there is a lovely orchard where my Grandpa and Lynn can commiserate over how to build the best bench for sitting under the leaves and soaking up the sunshine. Knowing them both, they probably won't take the time to rest on it.

The four E's, for being the best kids a mom could ever have. I'll never know how I got so lucky, but I'm grateful I did. You're my magnum opus.

William, for believing in me and my ability when I didn't, for seeing more in me than mud boots and manure stained jeans, for holding on and keeping me together when I fall apart, and for being the best decision I've ever made. You are the love of my life.

Table of Contents

Part III: Fruiting Wood

Forward

By William DeMille

Georgics

There is an old word, yet a new one to many, which Vernie and I have been using for years to describe the kind of farming we are engaged in. The Roman Poet Virgil used the word as the title to his famous poems of the land, its peasants, vines, grains, soils, livestock, and barns and a three-way partnership between man, nature, and the Gods; all working together in the act of bringing forth food from the harshness of nature. Yet people often view nature as pristine virgin beauty in contrast to Virgil's georgic message. It has been summed up that Georgics means: "enough work will conquer all [failure]." The Georgic ideal has sometimes taught that man must oppose nature, subdue her, harness her, and create order where no order existed before. But modern aesthetics show how much we love to see the pastoral view of untouched forests, crystal waterfalls, and geologic formation.

We, as georgic farmers, partner with the land and ask God to bless our efforts to secure a nutritious, abundant crop of culinary delights. We have always lived close to nature and enjoyed her pastoral gifts of sunrise and glistening dew, verdant meadows, snow capped peaks, rushing rapids, crashing surf, the vastness of the desert, and the majesty of scarlet sunsets. I find myself humbled and blessed by my partnership with Mother Nature as we have toiled together to

produce sweet fruits, succulent vegetables, savory herbs, and fragrant flowers.

Vernie and I have experienced a beautiful truth in our lives which we find has enhanced, not diminished, the partnership we have enjoyed with nature and production agriculture. We have not chosen the path of nature against man, farm against meadow, forest against field, or wetland against pasture. We have found that the opposition between the georgic and the pastoral views are just that: views. Not facts, not fiction, but simply the way someone understands it and how he or she writes it. These views exist as a means of understanding the truth of man and his relationship with nature and God. One is not good and the other bad—they are simply tools of the Great Debate in humanity's attempt to seek truth while we roam the earth.

We have realized from our agricultural existence that the Georgic and the Pastoral are simply two different sides of the same coin. We find beauty in work, and work is beautiful. We enjoy the gifts of nature, and we work to reproduce them. The fact that we work by no means diminishes the blossom. The blossom is often more beautiful because of the work. It is not a question of who is right between the Georgic view and the Pastoral. We need them both, not as two opposing poles, but as daily partners with every decision we make and every breath we take.

Georgics. Just a word but a word with substance. A descriptor. A title. A forgotten word in the rush of modern times. Forgotten like the thing it describes. Throughout known history people have forgotten what makes them great. They have exploited the greatness and have expected it to remain. Modern man has become great like so many great ages before us, and we too have forgotten how we arrived here. We have forgotten Georgics!

I am thrilled to introduce Walking My Fathers Fields to a hungry world in need of Georgic farmers. This work is an answer to prayers and an answer to feeding the hungry. Join

me in thanks to Vernie Lynn for giving us this awesome book which defines eloquently and brilliantly a new definition of what it really means to be Georgic.

Re-Writing History: An Author's Introduction

In the fall of 2009 I was living in a 130 year old adobe house in the beautiful Paradox valley in Southwestern Colorado with my husband William, my three boys Ezekiel, Ephraim, and Enoch, and my little girl Esther. We were farming a small 5 acre piece of borrowed land where we had erected five greenhouses, planted outside crops, and kept a small flock of chickens and pigeons. Every Tuesday and Thursday I loaded our beat-up mini-van and delivered farm fresh produce to Norwood and Telluride, Colorado and Moab and Monticello, Utah. We had moved there on April 22 of that year, my fourteenth wedding anniversary, and went right to work clearing fields, fixing up the house, and finding immense joy in participating in community events with our children in the tiny but tight community that thrived in that red soil. I didn't imagine life could ever get any better than that. It was the place I wanted to spend the rest of my life, raise my children, and grow old with my sweetheart.

I still think of it as a moment of perfection in a life that is often crazy, hard, thrilling, and beautiful.

I've come to believe that perfection is characterized by that kind of fleeting quality. I have spent my life pursing perfection of one sort or another. I love to travel for this reason. Perfection may lie just around the next bend, just past the far trees, or just a little further out from shore.

There in that old home, with some little birds that I didn't know the name of burrowing in the dried mud walls and squirrels living happily in the attic, I sat down with my pretty,

hand-bound journal and determined to write a book for my father who was turning 80 in November of that year.

As I began I had no clear idea of what the book would become; I just knew that I wanted to write it for both of my parents as a way of celebrating their well-lived lives and to share with them the things I learned growing up at their feet. For a long time I did nothing but sit cross-legged in my oversized, second-hand chair with the ugly upholstery, stare out the multi-paned window at the red cliffs and green alfalfa fields, chew up the end of my pen, and think.

I thought of my earliest memories. Of the farm fields and orchards, the cows, chickens, pigs, and horses that had filled the pastures of my first home. I thought of my mother's love of travel and my father's love for my mom that took us on a wider trip to see the farm fields of America and Canada, the miles of orchards, endless wheat fields, and valleys full of corn that introduced me to a world I hadn't known existed. I asked myself as I finally had to throw away the first chewed up pen "what do you remember about growing up on the farm and in the fields of America?"

This book grew from the answer to that question.

It began with a simple list of my favorite memories, or at least the memories that seemed most significant to me. I pondered them; I played around with a few story line ideas, and eventually got down to the business of writing down each memory.

But I'm a very distractible writer. I'd like to think I was simply a busy farmer and a mother to four children, but the truth is I'm just easily distracted. I found lots of reasons to not get my book done. There was the pumpkin patch adventure for the local school, there was the field trip up to Telluride, and then the other field trip to Telluride, and then there were the daily chores and the marketing for the new farm shares. There were the weekly deliveries, my graphic design side venture, volunteering once in awhile at the little charter

school in the valley, and visiting family in Eastland, Utah. Dad's birthday came and went, he got one story instead of a book, and time went on its merry way with no manuscript done.

In March of 2010 we left behind the perfect little valley of Paradox for a farming opportunity in Oregon that was too good to pass up. It broke my heart to say good-bye. I wept on the shoulder of one of my friends at church and told her that broken hearts must be God's way of making them just a little bit larger to let in more love.

At the time I felt that if I got any more love that way it would surely kill me.

We started work on the farm the first day we arrived in the Willamette Valley and for three and a half years we never stopped.

Except for once.

In October of 2010 William looked at me and asked "How's your book coming along?"

I hadn't been working on it for over six months. It was still in my mind and in my heart, I had several of the stories, my love letters, done, but it was nowhere near finished. I told him of my problem with distractions, told him I knew it was an excuse, but still a problem.

He just pursed his lips for a minute and said "I'm going to send you on a writing retreat. Why don't you call and make a reservation on the coast for three days. Turn off your phone, don't turn on the television, take your notebooks and your pens, and write your book."

I thought he was joking at first; I hadn't spent any of our meager income on anything that resembled a vacation and never on one just for me. I told him this and he just said "It's not a vacation, writing is work. This is a work trip."

So I called, made my reservation and that next Friday I set off, miraculously alone, for the Oregon Coast. I stopped at a grove of trees along the beach when I was almost to my destination and wrote "Jungle House" as I sat under the bower of storm battered branches and looked out at the crashing waves.

I kept driving, made it to the hotel which was nearly empty in the late season and wandered with my notebook in hand to the grass covered dunes to watch the sunset and wrote "Cider Press".

I finished about a third of the book over the weekend and set a pattern for the three weeks that followed, finally finishing the book and getting a manuscript done in time to send it out to my parents for Christmas that year.

And that was pretty much the end of the story. I had dreams of publishing it at some point, but that sounded terrifying. Thrilling of course, but horrifying at the same time. I looked into it a little which just served to scare me even more. I sent it off to people asking for feedback on how to make improvements. I sent it off to a few people to provide blurbs for the back cover in the event that someday I might actually attempt to have it published.

But there has always been something nagging at me, eating at the back of my mind and keeping me from really moving forward with putting this work in anyone else's hands.

Until tonight.

As my husband and I were coming home from visiting with family we were talking about the choices we make, particularly the choice we make to see the opportunities in our trials, the lessons in our lives. As we spoke I realized that there was a huge portion of the story that I had left out of this book, and it really needs to be here. I've told the story of growing up on the farm, how faith, love for family, the land, and my country shaped me, but that's really only part of the

tale. That's the part of the story that is past, a part I can't revisit except in memory.

What's missing is my future. Something happened to me as I wrote this work; something powerful, life altering, and profound. Something that I can learn from and utilize on a daily basis. There's a point in each of these love letters where I reveal a principle that I learned from an experience on the farm or during my travels to see the land of my birth. But I must confess that I never set out to share any principles. I just wanted to tell some stories from my perspective. The principles found me and they have altered the way I look at the world around me.

As I revisited my personal history, as I viewed through the lens of adulthood the experiences of youth, I finally understood why I believe the things I do, why I love the things I love, and what my own guiding principles are.

As I wrote my memories, I rewrote my history.

> And after the trials there is the joy, the strength, and those few and precious moments of perfection. Those golden drops of divine transcendence when the memories that hurt become the choices that heal.

So why does that make a difference to whomever reads this book?

Two reasons.

In this life there are two things that are uniquely ours. Two things which we share with no one else: our memories and our choices.

No one else in the world has experienced life in quite the same way that you have. Your memories tell who you have been, where you have come from, and what has made you the person you are; and no one can make your choices for you. Your choices determine what you do, where you are going, and what kind of person you will be.

17

This is a story of becoming; the story of a middle-aged farmer looking back at past harvests and looking forward to new crops and seasons.

This is the power of writing and the power of cultivation. It is constant and it is ever-changing, it is revelation and a curiosity, it is joy, sorrow, and the continuity of never-knowing and endlessly seeking. This is the promise that they make and the reason that I love them so: you will spend your life to make your mark upon the earth, to etch in stone that you were here, that you lived, loved, and tried your best to do something good with your days and the land will take your efforts like nourishing rain, the words you write will wing their way to the four corners of the globe, seasons will pass and like a tree in a forest your body will grow old, saplings will spring up at your feet, and in the end, like all good garden plants, what you leave behind at your death will nourish the plants, the people, and the world that carries on.

I wrote these love letters to my family, to the land that made me, to the faith that formed me, and to myself so that I would remember on the bleakest days that there have always been storms, there have always been sorrows, there have always been struggles. And after the trials there is the joy, the strength, and those few and precious moments of perfection. Those golden drops of divine transcendence when the memories that hurt become the choices that heal.

Lastly, this is my love letter to those who read, to those whose own story is full of the same journey. I hope that in reading this they will want to write me back, to tell their own story, to sing their own song. I believe that if enough of us tell our tales of hope that it will become what defines us as a people. There is strength in the everyday goodness of the men and women of my homeland. I long for the day when those are the stories I see in my mailbox.

Our life happens one moment at a time, our stories are told one word at a time. The choice is always before us to find in our days the beauty in the midst of the tragedy. Our

18

lives are a process of doing, doing, doing, growing, failing, progressing, and then there are moments; single, shining moments when in the midst of our efforts we reach understanding. In our understanding, in those fleeting seconds of clarity we gain the truths that sustain us, the principles that empower us to not just live but to enliven; to not simply age, but to grow in wisdom.

This is my story of choosing to see the majesty and beauty of divine love in the ordinary and mundane. We are all on a journey here, not to race with careless abandon toward a headstone in some green field, but to see with every step we take the spark of greatness in those we travel with. Our journey takes us through empty fields that we are called to cultivate, through silent homes which we are called to fill with laughter, and past hearts that labor beneath an unseen burden of pain that we might lift and lighten one another's load. Walk with me down slow paths, and find the peace that I have found in my father's fields.

Prologue

Arlington

Principle #1: Every Life is Important

I was 10 when we visited Arlington National Cemetery. Of course I'd been to a cemetery before; there was Oak Hill in San Jose, California where Grandpa Johnson was buried, which true to its name was covered in beautiful spreading oak trees; and there were the old Indian burial grounds behind our house in Northern California where the headstone of a Native American soldier killed in World War I stood alongside small metal markers engraved with names and nothing else. I walked to that cemetery often to run my fingers over the stone, the carved cross on the front, the aged granite, and the old bullet holes left by restless teenagers from years past. The burial ground never spooked me though the kids at Canyon Union Elementary would tell stories of wailing Indian ghosts and restless spirits. To me it was hallowed ground, a peaceful spot where I would sit in the warm summer sunshine of the Southern Cascades. It wasn't a well kept place by modern standards. The graves had collapsed into themselves, leaving indentations in the earth where the grass was flattened by sleeping deer. The wildflowers grew whichever way they wanted and the manzanita crept closer every year creating a bower beneath which the dead could sleep. It never bothered me, the wild, natural demeanor of the burial grounds; it actually seemed fitting somehow.

I don't know that I thought great thoughts while sitting there on that rocky red soil; it was just a pleasant place to rest after climbing the hill behind Kabyai Court. As my brothers can attest, my thoughts didn't range much beyond playing with my friend J.J. or which book I'd read last or what picture I was drawing. I had a happy little world: I was secure in my home, had plenty to eat, and my parents loved each other and me. They had instilled in me a love for the world around me and for the soil beneath my feet. I remembered working in the garden with them back on the "Apple Ranch," picking apples from beneath the trees for the cider press, or watching Mom bake bread or make cheese in the crock pot. A hundred different memories made up my love for the land at that time in my life, and all of them were pleasant.

Arlington changed that for me.

We had just come from visiting my brother Kirk at Fort Polk, Louisiana, and my brother Kris at Fort Jackson in South Carolina, where he was stationed for basic training, and had spent a day at Gettysburg as well. The thoughts of the war between brothers and my own brothers in the Army were fresh in my mind as we drove through those gates and saw Arlington for the first time.

It was such a marked difference from the little burial ground in Lakehead with its perfectly straight rows and well groomed grass. It was a crisp autumn day, not hot, not cold, just cool and perfect. I watched from the window as we passed the white headstones, row upon row like a perfectly planted field of corn or a well tended orchard; straight lines and diagonals crossing over themselves again and again. The number of headstones astounded me. Like the wheat fields of Kansas and the corn fields of Iowa, I was amazed by the sheer size and perfection of the placement.

We had come for no other reason than just to see it. We didn't bring a wreath for anyone. We didn't look for any one person or weep over a solitary grave. We had come to

see the place where our American dead had been given a place of honor.

"Our dead." That is how I thought of them. In all my memories of Arlington that is probably what stands out the most—the sense of common ownership. These fallen heroes, from the unknown soldiers to John F. Kennedy, were mine. This was the American hallowed ground—no bower of manzanita or wildflowers growing free, just rigid formality and an ideal perfection. We had no family that I knew of buried in that ground, but I felt the kinship nonetheless.

I stood beside my mother who watched, tears running down her face, as the changing of the guard at the Tomb of the Unknown Soldier took place. It was beautiful, the solemnity with which the guards took their place beside fallen comrades, the absolute firmness with which they stood at their post. It was seeing that young man stand there so straight and strong that changed something within me; my perception of the land began to shift, and memories of my time on the Ranch began to rearrange within my heart.

> I had never fully understood before that day that the peace we enjoyed on our farm, the pleasant memories of warm hay in the summer and spicy apples in the fall, had a price and that these young men were among the numbers who had paid it.

Here stood a young man, handsome and true in his dress uniform, next to the grave of another young man who had once stood straight and true as well. I had a very good imagination as a child, and I could easily see that soldier who, as the tomb says, was "known only to God" lying lifeless on a jungle floor or on a lonely beach or in a ravaged forest. I imagined another child like me waiting for a father or a brother who would never come home. What would it be like to never know? How would it change your life?

I stood there and remembered the love in my Grandfather's voice when he spoke of my brothers who were

serving, or who had served in the military. He was such a patriotic person, a man who saw his citizenship as a responsibility rather than a right; to him it was a sacred obligation. Something was working in me as I stood there, something profound and deep that I didn't have words to express.

We left the cemetery and traveled to the Mall in Washington D.C. We went to the top of the Washington monument. We saw the Smithsonian museums, and we went to the Wall.

It's an amazing monument really, similar to Arlington in its aesthetic principles: its sheer size, its clean lines, the black granite rather than the white, and the names. So many names. It is a symbol of the impact that the Vietnam War had on the whole country. I grew up in Northern California where the necessity of the war was still hotly debated, nearly a decade after it had ended, on street corners, in the post office lobby, or in grocery store aisles. The Wall represented it all. The volume of names told of how many American families were touched by the war. The black granite seemed to hold a wealth of grief for those who fought because their country said they needed to, for those who fought because they felt it was the right thing to do, and for those who didn't want to fight at all but had the courage to try to make the best of a bad situation.

I watched my mother weep again as she placed her hand against the cold granite and read names out loud. They weren't names she knew; she wasn't looking for a specific person. Once again the names were "our dead." These names were the common property of all Americans, the grief in the cold stone a common grief.

As I stood there, surrounded by the memory of life and death, the feelings that had begun to shift inside me at Arlington settled into a new shape, a new understanding, and nothing was common anymore. I recalled a conversation I had overheard between two men back home, reflecting their

anger at the waste of life in the war and the pointless deaths of so many soldiers. I remembered their words, and it made me angry.

Like my mother I placed my hand against the cold, dark granite, and I felt in my heart the truth that came out of my mouth that day: "Your life was not a waste; your death was not pointless. I'm here; I'm free, and I remember."

For the first time in my life I understood why my parents loved the land so much, why they prayed over crops and wept over lost farm animals. I had never fully understood before that day that the peace we enjoyed on our farm, the pleasant memories of warm hay in the summer and spicy apples in the fall, had a price and that these young men were among the numbers who had paid it. The men and women that slept beneath the green fields at Arlington had paid it; the youths whose blood had reddened the meadow at Gettysburg had paid it; my own brothers were enlisted and would pay for our peace with their time and lives if necessary.

Every name on that wall mattered; every name on those white stones at Arlington mattered. Not one sacrifice was a waste; not one life lost was unappreciated. I stood there in the cool autumn sunshine, and my love for the land deepened. My appreciation for the ability to watch the seasons, the sowing and reaping, increased. I have never forgotten it.

This book is in part my letter of thanks, my witness to the families of our dead that they are remembered, loved, and appreciated—that their sacrifice has not gone unnoticed and that even the soldiers whose names are known only to God have a place in my heart.

It is because of them that I am free to walk my father's fields.

Part One

Roots

Hillcrest Orchards

Principle #2: It is my responsibility to love and care for the land

My earliest memory is of bathing several small kittens in an old tire swing that hung from a tree in the front yard of our home in Northern California. Our place was called Clark Creek; we always seem to live in homes that have names. I'm not sure if this was my Mom's doing or if the names already existed. It was a big, beautiful old home built in the 19-teens. It had served as a mountain gambling and drinking retreat during the prohibition years for some of California's most colorful people. It boasted large rooms, a huge fireplace, and a wrap-around, all-season porch. It didn't seem to mind settling down with a quiet family who didn't drink, smoke, or carouse. It was a bit like an old man who had enjoyed his heyday but was settled now and content to relive his wild past with nothing more than stories.

The kitten memory is somewhat disturbing as I can't seem to remember whether or not I ever removed them from the swing. I'm hoping that I did, but since I was three at the time there is simply no telling.

My next memory is as clear as a bell in my mind. I remember sitting on my father's lap while he drove the old diesel tractor out through the sunny hay meadow. I still remember that smell of warm hay and diesel exhaust. I felt as safe, secure, and loved as could be.

We moved from Clark Creek a little over a year from when we moved in. My parents had left behind the hustle and

bustle of San Jose nearly two years earlier, and they were still searching for what they wanted. I can't speak for them, but I think in the backs of their minds they were searching for "more." Not more money, not a better job, but rather more time for family, more land, and more open space. They found it outside a small Cascade Mountain town called Montgomery Creek.

An apple ranch by the name of Hillcrest Orchards was for sale. It had been there for at least 50 years. It had grandfathered water rights, apple tree varieties that weren't even being sold anymore, an apple cider press, and what we called the "Apple Shanty" along a highway just a mile or so away, where the produce from the ranch was sold every year. My sister fell in love with it and wanted to buy it.

It's important at this point to get an idea of my family dynamics. We were a true yours, mine, and ours family. I was the youngest of a combination of four different families, resulting in 12 children all together. I believe that it is a credit to my parents that while growing up, I never

> It is hard for me to contemplate a life where feet and hands never touch the dirt. It is like air and water, as necessary to life as breathing.

viewed any of my brothers and sisters as half's or steps. I have never loved any of my brothers or sisters halfway. Some were already grown, married, and had children of their own by the time I came along, but I was raised knowing that we were a family. We didn't just belong to one parent or another; we belonged to each other. So it wasn't such a strange thing for my sister, who was eighteen years older than I, to suggest that we buy a farm.

I think my parents had a better idea of the work that would be involved in the running of the farm than my sister did. My father had lived his childhood through the Great Depression on a farm in rural Utah, and my mother, though she grew up in the middle of San Jose, had had a great deal of

experience with raising her own food in her parents' backyard during the rationing of World War II.

They fell in love with the farm also. We all did. Even to this day when we get together, we talk about the "Ranch" as if it were just yesterday.

After my husband and I had been married for a year or so, he said to me, "From the way all of you talk about the Ranch, I thought you grew up there. You were only there for four years!"

Time is relative I guess. Those were the four years that have had the biggest impact on my life. It set the foundation for how I've looked at everything since.

It was at Hillcrest Orchards that I remember riding on my father's lap in the orchard meadow. I have to be honest here and say that I don't remember too much of the logistics of the farm as my memories are those of a very young child. But young as I was there were a few things that I learned then that have stuck with me through all the rest of my days. I learned some important things on that farm: don't walk in a field with a Jersey bull with only your 6-year-old brother for protection, don't fall in the goose pen, you can't rush a grandma, don't put your face by the dog's teeth and then put your knee on his foot. I have a good memory when it comes to things that happened nearly 30 years ago. My brothers still tease me that I could find my way down a back country road because I'll see a daisy growing along a ditch bank and remember it. I may not remember a conversation I had with my husband some two days past, but I remember my childhood well. I sometimes worry about early-onset Alzheimer's or maybe I'm just getting old.

It's fascinating now as an adult to watch my children interact with one another and see how the things we do as a family affect them. The most interesting thing to me is how we can do one thing together and they will talk about it for months afterward saying things like "Mom, remember how we

31

used to always play at Snail Park?" (We went there maybe five times in five years.) Or "remember how I used to make breakfast for everyone when we were on the farm?" (They helped their Dad make pancakes a couple of times.) Seeing them do that I'm forced to admit that my memories are probably colored with the same kind of brush. I remember going to the movie theater in Burney, California, in my pajamas. I used to think that we did that all the time, but since the only movie I can remember seeing is Bedknobs and Broomsticks, there's a really good chance that we only did that once. It makes me want to make sure to do good things with my children. If they are going to distort the memories anyway, why not lean them a little to the happy side?

Hillcrest Orchards is where I spent the days of my earliest memories. Its hills, trees, forests, and streams are tied up with my perceptions of family, faith, and friends. It's impossible to separate my love of family from my love of that land; they are too intertwined with one another.

I've found that it can be difficult to explain this deep love for what some consider just a bunch of dirt to anyone who hasn't experienced it themselves. People in general understand the concept of loving your home; after all you live in it, try to make it pleasant, and create family memories in it. But the land is more than that. It's not just the memories created on it, not just the crop that decorates it, not just the minerals that stain it red or black, or the smell of it when the warm summer rain hits it. It's all those things and more. It's all the crops that will be grown over the next hundred years. It's all of the memories that you have and all the memories that you plan to have. For a farmer it's the sum of life's labor. "For dust thou art, and unto dust shalt thou return" (Gen. 3:19). This is not a declaration of grief for a farmer; it is a testimony of our place in the cycles of the Earth. Anyone who tends the soil and the treasures that grow from it understands the cycle of life and death. I learned as a child and I have taught my own children that everything lives because something else died. That is the gift and responsibility of life. The grass and plants live because millions of microbes in the

soil have fed off of the decaying organic matter of hundreds of plants and animals, died themselves, and provided food for the roots of the living plants. All living things owe their existence to the soil, and someday our own bodies will feed the soil from whence we take our living.

It is hard for me to contemplate a life where feet and hands never touch the dirt. It is like air and water, as necessary to life as breathing. The love for the land goes beyond mere affection or aesthetic appeal. It is not something that can be appeased by a title of ownership for acreage. It must be tended, cherished, and sacrificed for. It must be reverenced and never taken for granted. It must be taken to task sometimes and amended and corrected in order to reach full productivity. It must be beautified and enjoyed. That is love for the land.

A friend of mine who has made the study of Native American culture a huge part of her life told me once of a remarkable Navajo tradition. She said "The Navajo people teach that if you are angry or sad or simply frustrated with life, you must take off your shoes and walk outside barefoot. Once you are outside, you stand on the bare earth with your bare feet and allow all the negativity within you to drain out through the soles of your feet and be swallowed up by the soil and instead take from the earth all the positive energy of life and growing." I love that concept, that we are participants with the Earth, capable of giving and receiving from her goodness. Farmers have the same belief. Just like the old gardener's saying, "You can bury a lot of troubles while digging in the dirt."

These are the roots that sank deep in the soil of Hillcrest Orchards. Could I have told you all of this by the time I left the ranch at 7 years old? No, I don't believe I could have. But after a lifetime of looking forward and looking back, I can see that the way my life has grown was in part determined by the way I was planted and tended at that tender age in the fertile soil of the orchard. I come from the dirt and someday I will return thereto, but in between that eternal planting and

reaping are many harvests. I have seen enough to know that I want more. This is not greed, it is love. There are crops I have yet to raise, fields I have yet to tend. This is the responsibility that every farmer feels. It is what drives us on year after year even when it costs more to plant the seeds than we will ever get for the harvested crop. It is what drives us on even when we are driving the tractor under the hot August sun and thinking, "I should have been a banker." It is what comforts us on cold December evenings when we look out at the snow covered fields and dream of what we will grow next spring. It is a love that we give freely to the soil and is returned again and again to us in harvest and hope.

Nana's Aprons

Principle #3: Live in such a way that when others hear your name they know that it means "love"

My mom is known by multiple names. There's Nana, Grandma, Mom, Momnwie, Jan, Painie and Grandma Jan. But regardless what name she is known by to her family and friends, when we think of her, it is always associated with smiles, laughter, and aprons.

My mom has two hobbies. She reads and she cooks. She is in heaven when the latest Taste of Home magazine arrives in her mailbox because it is such a fantastic marriage of those two pursuits. I moved 1,200 miles away from her and Dad's farm a few years ago, and she still calls me to tell me the latest recipe she tried and how she plans to amend it and make it her own. I love the continuity of Mom. I could walk into her house on any day of the week, at anytime of that day, and find her in one of two places: the kitchen, stirring something that smells superb on the stove, or the den, sitting in her favorite chair surrounded by piles of books and magazines.

The love of good food started when my Mom was very young. Her father, my Grandpa Stratton, was injured in an accident during the WWII era in San Jose, California. His injury necessitated Grandma Stratton's return to the workforce. Mom has told me often she can remember running to greet Grandma as she walked home from the bus stop in her pretty work clothes and then watching her in the evenings as she

would take off her beautiful lace-trimmed blouse and stockings, wash them out and hang them to dry for the next day's work, make dinner for the family and attend to household chores. She watched this day in and day out over several years, and as she grew older she observed how tired her mother was, how weary at the end of the day she sometimes seemed, and my mother wanted to help. She told me once how she remembers asking Grandma when she was washing out her pretty blouse one evening, "Mama, what can I do to help you? What can I do to make things easier?" If you knew my Mom you would smile at that question; it has defined her life. She has spent years perfecting that desire to make life better for others. And I think it all started in that little house in San Jose in 1946. Grandma Stratton didn't brush off my Mom's question; she knew that she meant it and she took her seriously. She took my mother's hands in hers and said, "Janice, if you could learn how to cook, it would help me a lot. If you could start dinner when you get home from school, it would save me a lot of time."

So that is what my Mom did. She says there were a few big mistakes early on, the most memorable being the time she used Tabasco sauce on the salad thinking it was vinegar dressing. Uncle Cecil thought he was going to die; but, other than the rare near-death kitchen experiences, cooking seemed to come naturally to her. She followed her mother's advice; and when she got home from school, she would help start dinner. Her own grandmother, my Great-Grandma Stowe, lived not far away and according to my mother she was a superior cook. Everyone wanted to celebrate holidays at "Mamie's" house and enjoy her cooking. She never bought anything canned; she was truly a "from scratch" cook. She taught my Mom the secret to good gravy, how to ensure that the meat wasn't

> Problems are ever present,
> but it helps
> to step back from them sometimes,
> take a few minutes to find joy
> in the love of family
> and bask in its warmth.

over-cooked, how to check produce for quality, and all about aprons.

I have just two pictures of Great-Grandma Stowe when she was a grown woman, and she is wearing an apron in both of them. Her aprons are similar to the ones my Mom wears now, more of a smock than a skirt, with arm and neck holes, strings to tie in the back and deep pockets. When she woke in the morning, she would dress and put on her apron first thing. It was her uniform, her armor, and the insignia of her rank. There was no discouragement in wearing that apron. There was no regret for roads untraveled or songs unsung. There was no feeling of drudgery wrapped up in wearing that well-used cloth. I'm sure there were moments of frustration that had her propping her hands on her hips and wearing the fabric there a little thin, probably more than a few tears (her own and others) wiped with the hem, and countless childhood treasures housed in the pockets.

I never knew Great-Grandma Stowe. She died when my mother was in her teens. It was a hard loss for her. She loved her Grandma; she was her rock when her father was injured and was in the hospital for over a year---a hospital that didn't allow children inside for visits. Grandma Stowe did what so many dedicated grandparents do; she softened all the rough edges of living. She wrapped my mother up in her arms and rocked her when her heart was filled with fear and worry, wiped her eyes with her apron, then took her hand and led her into the kitchen where she could put both of their hands to work and ease some of the heartache. There was nothing she could do to heal the wounds of my Mom's father, but she could heal some of her granddaughter's hurt. With a little cup of flour, a pinch of salt, and some sugar and spice she could make something warm and sweet to try to ease a little of the cold of fear inside. There's something to be said for setting your cares aside for a moment to enjoy a homemade cookie and a cup of "silver tea", a drink made of milk with a spoonful of tea and sugar in it, as my mother did in her Grandma's kitchen. Problems are ever present, but it helps to step back

from them sometimes, take a few minutes to find joy in the love of family and bask in its warmth.

There was so much more to Great-Grandma Stowe's daily teatime ritual than biscuits and a warm drink. There was the continuity of family: no matter what. There was the love of simple pleasures in the face of any obstacle. There was the understanding that she couldn't make everything "all better," but she could provide just a little physical and emotional nourishment every day. By taking the time to not only teach my mother how to cook, but how to enjoy what she had made, Great-Grandma Stowe showed my mother that her worth went far beyond the work she did in the kitchen or the house. The work became not drudgery but rather an expression of love for one another. It was a gift from the heart, worked with their hands, and given freely. It is a lesson my mother has never forgotten.

When my Mom married my Dad after the tragic death of his first wife Birgit, she knew it would not be an easy thing to blend two different families, with different cultures, different memories, and still so much pain and loss in everyone's hearts. One of the first things she found after they were married was an apron that had belonged to Birgit. It was a lovely thing and wonderfully practical, evidence of a mother who had loved her children enough to make their home beautiful and to find joy in that service. Mom's Aunt Bernice, who was a good seamstress, saw the apron she was wearing and took it home to re-create it. The next Christmas Mom got a package in the mail that held 3 new aprons.

Wearing an apron may seem like a small thing, but it is so like my mom to have thought of it. She wanted to provide a sense of continuity to all the children. She didn't seek to replace their Mother, but rather to provide them with simple reminders of her influence on our family. She couldn't heal all their hurts, but she could show them that they were loved, that their traditions, their mother's traditions, were still alive and treasured. She couldn't take away the pain that death had struck in their hearts, but she could create a meal that

would warm them a little and provide them with the nourishment they needed to keep going until things got a little better. My sister Debbie told me once that even before Mom and Dad were married all the kids looked forward to Thursday nights because that's when Jan would bring over dinner and cookies. She said, "There were other church women who would bring over things like onion casserole with peas. Who brings stuff like that to a bunch of kids? It's disgusting. But your mom would bring hot dogs or potato casserole with lots of cheese and cookies every time. We loved it when Jan came over with dinner."

The older I get, the more I am amazed at the depth of love my Mom has showered on her family. I grew up knowing and loving family that I never met. She hung pictures of Birgit on the wall so that everyone who visited would know the lovely woman whom my Dad had loved and raised a beautiful family with. She told me once when I was looking at the pictures as a young teenager, "When I married your Dad, I often thought to myself, 'How would I want to be remembered?' and I have tried to always keep memories of Birgit around our home. She loved your Dad, your Dad loved her, and she is a part of our family. I would want to be remembered too." And so I grew to love a woman I never met, but to whom I owe a huge debt of gratitude. She gave me many of my brothers and sisters, she is the grandmother of some of my best friends ever, and she holds a place of honor, respect, and love in my heart because of the tenderness of my own mother's heart.

And so my mom was able to take a simple thing, an apron, and weave two families' histories together with it. I've heard her tell the story of where her apron pattern came from to Birgit's granddaughters and then tell them the story of her Grandma Stowe's aprons because they are her granddaughters also. Remember, there are no half's or steps in our family. Every year Aunt Bernice sent Mom a package with new aprons in it, all in a multitude of colors. Whenever the next generation was learning to sew, an apron was always on the list of things to make. My Mom has worn them all. She

39

saves the prettiest ones for her Sunday best just like Great-Grandma Stowe used to do; she color coordinates them to match whatever she's wearing that day. She has shared them with her Amish neighbors, and they've become a huge hit in the community. The local Amish women's industrious fingers have sewn enough aprons to cover most of Harrison County.

A small and simple thing...a worn piece of green paisley cloth fastened with a button in the back. But not so small when I think that my Mom took that little cloth apron brought from Sweden over half a century ago with Birgit and tied it to the apron string traditions of the Stratton's, Stowe's, Putnam's and Inman's and wrapped all of us up in a legacy of love, daily dedication to one another, and a treasury of small joys that have led to a lifetime of happiness.

The name she goes by in each part of our family doesn't seem to matter much; it is what the name has come to mean that has made all the difference. Come visit sometime, and I can show you where love lives and how she dresses. No matter what time of day it is I can guarantee you she'll be in an apron.

Nipper

Principle #4: Don't put limits on love, it is boundless

Every farm needs a dog. They fill a multitude of roles on the homestead: shepherd, cowhand, chief guard, nursemaid, gatekeeper, playmate, companion, and occasionally lifeguard. Their intelligence is remarkable, the quality of their listening skills is unparalleled, and their affection is unconditional and unending. My son is currently in search of a border collie. We went camping this summer with my brother Christer and his sweet wife Leilani. She has a border collie named Shay. Ezekiel saw her and was instantly in love. He's on the internet daily looking at working dogs, breed lines, tips for training a cow or sheep dog, and what to look for in an animal that will be both laborer and friend.

Animals are everywhere on a working farm. We have cows, chickens, ducks, geese, pigs, horses, goats, one bunny, turkeys, a barn cat named Midnight complete with kittens, and a barn cat who thinks she's a house cat named Isis. Our friends, the Olsen's, who work with us on the farm, have a one-eyed golden retriever named Rusty who has become a kind of farm mascot. We're so glad they brought him when they came. The farm just wasn't complete without his wagging tail and slobbery greetings.

There is such simple satisfaction in sitting down at the end of the day with a dog curled up beside you, his head resting on your leg. He takes a deep breath and lets out a huge sigh that says it all: "Ahh...the end of another productive

41

day. Isn't it great?" I've sat in harmony like that many times, feeling the gentle give and take of canine affection.

We always had a dog while I was growing up. There was Becky, Blue, Nipper, Major, Penny, Buttons, and Pugsley. Becky was a golden lab who lived with us at Hillcrest Orchards. She was a friendly, sweet-tempered, and talented pooch. Unfortunately her greatest talent was gathering eggs. She would trot up to the hen house and gather up to six at a time in her mouth. If we could have trained her to bring them directly to the kitchen this would have been fine but she usually brought them to the porch, spat them out into a row, and then proceeded to eat them. This is not generally considered acceptable behavior in a farm dog and so we had to find an egg-free home for Becky. Blue was, as you might expect, a blue heeler cow dog. I've often wondered how many blue heelers there are in the United States named "Blue" and pondered why such an unoriginal name persists across North American ranches to this day. Blue was part of a cow herding partnership with Nipper who was a header. As a heeler Blue would approach the cows or pigs from behind and use yips, growls, and barred teeth to move them where she wanted them to go. As the header Nipper would direct the herd left and right as they moved along.

Major was a Great Dane so big and so gentle that I could ride around the living room on his back. He and Nipper didn't get along very well so he had to find a new home as well. Penny was a Chihuahua that came with the borrowed Winnebago that took us around the United States. We babysat her for the summer, but she was already attached to another family so she mostly just tolerated us in her space. Then there was Buttons, a sweet and sassy Boston Terrier, who was our best friend for the better part of a decade. We taught her to howl at the TV whenever the Nestle Tollhouse cookie advertisements came on. "Please don't eat all the moooorsels (howl) please don't eat them alllllll! (howl) 'Cause if you eat all the moooorselllls (howl, howl, howl) the cookies (howl) will be (howl) ballllld!" She would keep howling for a good five minutes after that. It was funny but made watching

MacGyver a little difficult. We taught her how to be an attack dog—with Mom's throw pillows. She was a terrifying little thing when she wanted to be; her eyes would almost glow green when she saw a pillow coming near her slowly. She was the perfect companion for afternoon naps on lazy days. We mourned for ages when she died, and she is buried in a place of honor beneath the golden forsythia outside Mom's kitchen window in Missouri.

Pugsley was my dog, a roly-poly, snuffly Chinese pug that we acquired by accident from my sister-in-law Joy's parents when Dad and I made the final move from California to Missouri in 1991. They were fostering her until she could find a permanent home, and she found one with us. She was, depending on the day, Buttons' best friend or worst enemy. They competed all day for attention and snuggled down in perfect harmony every night. She was dognapped just a few years after we got her, and it was a terrible loss.

I enjoyed all of our dogs, each one was a friend, but it was Nipper who taught us all about second chances and selfless dedication.

> I love that about dogs.
> They know you're being stupid but they come along to keep you company and try to protect you as best they can anyway.
> I love cats too,
> but they are above stupidity.

He came to us in the beat-up cab of the local veterinarian's work truck on one of the routine visits he made to the farm. He had found Nipper in a room full of dogs that were scheduled to be euthanized. A farmer had brought them in, swearing that they were all chicken killers. This news was the death knell for a dog in serious farm country because no farmer will risk not only his own livelihood but that of his neighbors as well with a dog that kills for pleasure. The vet told my mom, "I don't know why, but I just took one look at this old guy and knew he wasn't a killer." He hadn't wanted to see him put down so he took him home, but as the owner of several dogs already he was on the lookout for a farm family who could give him a permanent home.

43

So Nipper came to live at Hillcrest Orchards. He was a Queensland/McNab cross, with the herding instinct alive and well in his blood. Some dogs in the working breed class have been bred to be more pet than partner but it wasn't true of Nipper. He had an uncanny ability to sense where he was needed on the farm at any given moment. One of my first memories of him was as a companion and guard dog. My dad and two of my brothers, Kirk and Kris, were out in the forest past the far pasture cutting up downed trees for firewood. My brother Jared and I wanted to go help. There was a road that we could have taken to get out to the forest. It ran past the barn and the hog shed and on into the pines, but apparently as a five and six year old we were convinced that this would take too long. So we opted, very unwisely, to instead go through the pasture that housed Knuckles, the Jersey bull.

We had acquired Knuckles as a day-old calf from a local dairy farmer who didn't need a bull calf and didn't have time to correct his birth defect that gave him his name; clubbed hooves. They were so badly turned under that he couldn't stand at all, but my dad worked with him every day, massaging his legs, stretching the hooves, and eventually getting them pulled far enough to allow for splints to be placed on his legs. He learned to walk and then run. He grew into a fine, large, healthy Jersey bull.

If you've never lived around dairy farmers, I should probably tell you here that there is a reason, beyond the expense of caring for an animal, that they don't always own a bull even though reproduction is an essential aspect of their operation. Dairy bulls are mean—not in a malicious way (like geese for example, those harmless looking spawn of the Devil); they are just built to be the protectors of their herd, and they take their job seriously. They don't like anyone to come near their girls and they keep a watchful eye on anyone who gets too close. My Grandpa Stratton used to tell us that growing up in Wisconsin they would hear at least once a year about someone in their area who was killed or injured by a bull because of carelessness. My mom and dad had very strict

rules about the bull and his pasture. Never, never, never, NEVER go in the pen with Knuckles.

Why do young people think that rules don't apply to them? And not just family specific rules, but societal rules and even physical laws seem to be like a personal challenge issued to youth.

Jared and I completely ignored our parent's stricture concerning the bull pasture; we thought if we walked slow enough, kind of sneaky and stealthy like, he wouldn't notice us. I remember thinking, as I swung my leg over the top rung of the fence railing and saw Knuckles watching us, his tail flicking from side to side and his head lowered, "This is not a very good idea." A truer observation could not be found.

We started walking, creeping really, past the bull while he stood there, snorting at us and keeping his eyes on us the whole time. I am grateful to say that we didn't find out if he would have charged us or not because we had gone no farther than five feet into the pen when a well-muscled brown and black fur ball came sailing over the fence and landed beside us. Nipper had joined us on our little trip into insanity.

I love that about dogs. They know you're being stupid but they come along to keep you company and try to protect you as best they can anyway. I love cats too, but they are above stupidity. They'd just as soon lick their paws and watch you from the fence post with an air of superiority that says "You'll not see me try that, you lunatic."

We walked on together; Nipper on the far side of Jared, closest to Knuckles, and me on the other side glancing over at the bull every few minutes as we crept along. I remember Jared saying, "Now don't run, we don't want to startle him." But he never once offered to come after us. Nipper didn't even have to growl at him or bare his teeth. Knuckles had experienced what tangling with Nipper meant, and I don't think that he was interested in pursuing that course of action again. He had once cornered my dad by the

fence near the barn where he'd been putting out hay for the cows. But Knuckles wasn't interested in hay, he was out for blood. He charged and sent my dad flying through the air. He hollered out "Nipper" before he even hit the ground and in almost less than a heartbeat Nipper was there, feet splayed, hair up, and his chest rumbling with a truly frightening growl. Knuckles was feeling pretty full of himself that day, and he went after Nipper; but as a header cow dog Nipper wasn't the kind of canine that would tuck tail and dodge. As soon as the bull put his nose down to try and fight the dog that was between him and his prey, Nipper dashed in and bit him square on the nose. He was too fast and too smart to get stomped or head-butted. Knuckles bellowed, Nipper growled and barked, and it gave my dad enough time to pick himself up and get out of the pen as fast as he could. As soon as dad was safe, Nipper came leaping out of the pen again, tail wagging, tongue lolling, panting and grinning the way dogs do when they know they've done something great.

No, Knuckles didn't offer to come after us; we made it safely to the forest thanks to Nipper's watchful care. He was the farm equivalent of the Captain of the Guard, and he took his duty to keep the farm and his family safe very seriously.

A neighbor of ours, Joan, once told my mom "Jan, Nipper is not the same dog when you're gone from home. He's friendly when you're there, but when you aren't, nobody gets past him." She then recounted how she'd driven down the long driveway onto the ranch and had seen Nipper jump off the porch and race down to the front gate. She called our "Hey Nipper!" but apparently our protector was unmoved by a friendly voice. He just sat there, no tail wagging and a hard look in his eyes. Joan tried walking a little bit closer to the house but Nipper put his ears back and rumbled out a low growl from deep in his chest. She thought it best to just climb back into her vehicle and wait for Nipper to get tired of guarding the porch and front door. A few minutes went by while she was sitting in the cab of her truck, and Nipper disappeared from the gate that led into the yard so she opened up her door and prepared to get out. But Nipper

hadn't gone very far; he was lurking underneath the truck like a shark waiting to move in for the kill. He caught Joan's boot heel in his mouth when she stepped out and nearly gave her a heart attack. She decided she'd try visiting the farm again later when my mom and dad were home.

Nipper was an essential member of our farm family. We all loved him. Mom would try to bring him inside to sleep sometimes especially whenever it was cold. But he never wanted to. He'd sit at the door and whine, agitated that he couldn't be out in the barn, watching out for the other animals. As soon as Mom opened the door for him, he would take off for the hay loft and sleep there completely at peace with his place in the world.

I've done my own searching for a border collie since Ezekiel has started looking for one. I've been reading about their behavior and their intelligence. I've looked into dog adoption services to see if there are any working dogs out there. I came across an ad for an Australian shepherd named Max that pulled at my heartstrings. Max had lived on a farm, but his owners had moved and couldn't take him with them. They'd entrusted him to foster care until a good farm home could be located. It made me think of Nipper—once a farm dog, always a farm dog.

It was one of our biggest struggles when we left the ranch, what do we do with the dogs? Blue found a home with a neighbor, but Nipper was a one family, one farm dog. Mom and Dad wrestled with what to do with him. We didn't want to give him away; we wanted Nipper with us. He came with us to Burney, California, which was a 6-month stopgap for our family between selling the ranch and finding a new farm. But when we set out in the motor home, we knew he couldn't go on such a long road trip. The confinement would drive him crazy. So we decided that Nipper would stay with Grandma and Grandpa Stratton in their San Jose Jungle House while we were gone for the summer.

He tolerated it, but he didn't like it. Grandma would sit in the backyard petting him for hours, but she still felt guilty when she went in the house. He needed room to run and work to do. He was just too active a dog to be kept in a city.

When we got back to California, we still hadn't found a farm. We were staying in the motor home and had no room for Nipper yet. Mom and Dad started searching for a place for him and finally found it with Chuck and Kathy Marriott, my sister-in-law Joy's parents. Chuck supervised the school farm down in Redding, and he had the room and the work to keep a healthy farm dog occupied. We moved Nipper up there, and he seemed to settle in well. We were happy that he seemed content, that he wasn't cooped up and anxious anymore from lack of labor.

We weren't expecting to get a call from Chuck months later telling us that Nipper had disappeared from the farm. They'd looked for him everywhere, but he wasn't to be found. We speculated on where he might be, where he could have gone, and we worried for him. My mom said to me one day, "I've read that a dog can only stand three homes; they can't endure being shuffled around so much. They're just made to stick with one family, one home." She thought that Nipper may have run away from the school farm in an effort to go back to Hillcrest Orchards to find what he had been taken away from.

I imagined him, that dear friend and protector, climbing mountains and crossing rivers to try to get back to the ranch and his family that wasn't there anymore. I wished we could be there for him. I wished he could come home and find the farm unchanged from when he had stood guard there. We never heard what happened to him. If he made it to the ranch, he didn't stay long enough for anyone to see him. It's more likely that he never made it out of Redding, but how I wish he did. Even if he couldn't make it "home," I wish for him that he found the woods and the wild again. I wish for him that he raced under spice-scented pine trees and drank

from clean mountain streams until he found a place where he could live in peace and satisfaction.

I read once, "Heaven is the place where every dog you've ever loved runs to lick your face." If you have ever loved a dog, you know the hope this sentiment expresses. Nipper saved the lives of my family members more than once. He gave us his love and devotion with no strings attached and without thought of repayment. He forgave when offended and loved when insulted. As a dog he lived more fully the ideal we aspire to as people. He expressed more charity, faith, and in the end hope than some people ever experience. I can't help but hope for myself that I will see him again, that we will run together through green pastures, unafraid of mean dairy bulls and abandonment, just two friends who love one another in spite of differences in appearance, language, and species. Two friends whose souls are bound together by love, because love knows no limits and love has no end.

Cider Press

Principle #5: Hold on and allow yourself to be held

Apples were our focus at Hillcrest Orchards. We had hundreds of trees, dozens of varieties, and a dedication to quality. The ranch sat on a back road off of the two-lane highway that linked Redding to Susanville and all of the small towns in between. There was no traffic on Old Cove Road, and no one would have stopped to buy apples if they had to go so far to get them. This is a common problem among the farms of America: people don't want to smell the farms in their backyards or be woken up by their tractors in the wee hours of the morning or middle of the night, but they don't want to drive to the country to purchase their goods either. Our problem was solved by the Apple Shanty that sat out on the two-lane about three miles away. People stopped by all through the season to purchase apples, pears, some twenty-five cent refrigerator drawings I offered for sale, and apple cider. Long-time customers, the ones who had been purchasing from the orchard since before we owned it, would drive for hours just to come to the shanty to pick up gallons of fresh-pressed, unpasteurized apple cider.

Cider is best when it's fresh and icy cold. We had a large, walk-in cooler at the shanty that mom kept it in. I loved it when she would take out the bottles to offer samples. It was cold, sweet, and spicy. It tasted of summer with just a touch of frosty fall. There was nothing else like it in all the world. The dusky taste of it was like nectar. Mom would freeze it so that we could enjoy the fresh taste later on in the

dead of winter when we were buried in the mountain snowfall and apple harvests seemed light years away.

Occasionally we would have a bottle that wouldn't sell soon enough, and an old neighbor of ours would come up to the back of the store and ask my mom, "Do you have any of the good stuff? I'd like to make some vinegar with it." Mom would give him a bottle or two for free, and come in shaking her head, "Vinegar...right. That old guy's making hooch up there in the mountains." I didn't have any idea what "hooch" was but I figured it wasn't good. Occasionally the cider would go hard all on its own, even in the cooler. One Halloween my dad took several bottle of what he thought was fresh cider to the local church harvest party where he donned a huge pumpkin and told "Headless Horseman" stories for all of the delightfully spooked kids. We kept going back for more and more cider, which had a nice little tingle to it. Finally, after we all kept getting sillier and sillier as the night progressed, one of the adult women in charge sniffed the cider and tasted a little bit.

"Vern Johnson!" she exclaimed. "This cider's gone hard! You've gotten them all drunk! What on earth will their parents say?!" I don't know about the other kids or their parents but I always thought it was a memorable night.

Of course good cider has to start with good apples. Mom has always claimed that our cider was so good because of the wonderful array of heirloom apples we had available for the mix. The whole process would begin in the orchard, out under the leaves of the trees and the warm mountain sunshine. Every member of the farm family helped with apple harvest. Even I, the smallest member of the family, helped with bringing in the apples. My dad would strap a harvesting bag onto me, it was almost as tall as I was, with a thick upper edge, banded with metal that kept it open all the time, and an open bottom that clipped up or down depending on whether you wanted to fill or empty it. My job was simple: pick up any windfall that was not bruised and damaged. There is always windfall when you have fruit trees. It's a natural process that

can nicely thin fruit, or destroy an entire harvest if the winds are too strong. Beginning in spring, as soon as the apples start to form on the branches, the small unripe fruit will bump against each other, rub against the branch, and occasionally come loose to fall to the earth in a self-composting heap. I was living in Monticello, Utah, a couple of years ago when a neighbor stopped by and asked if he could harvest our  apricots since we were just letting them fall on the ground to waste. William told him that they weren't ripe enough to harvest yet, and the man continued to argue that they were ripe enough to fall off so surely they were ripe enough to be harvested. William explained to him about windfall, but he still thought we were wasting the fruit. I tried not to be offended but I'm not sure I was successful since I'm still irritated about it.

It was my job to pick up these windblown fruits. I can remember walking among the downed apples, looking for whole fruit, unmarred and still good among the pungent, sweet-spicy fragrance of the apples already decaying on the ground. Every one I found was a treasure. I'd hold them up to show Mom and Dad or Kris. "Good job!" they'd say and

continue their endless task of climbing up and down the three-legged ladders into the heights of the apple trees. I was so jealous of Aaron and Jared because they were big and strong enough to help with actual tree harvests. I would never have been able to do it of course; I don't think I did much windfall harvesting either to be honest. My parents would probably have let the windfall stay on the ground if I hadn't been out there wanting to help. But they knew how important it was for a child to feel that her work was essential to the family, to feel needed and appreciated. I felt good about the work I did.

When the trailer and bushel baskets were filled to the brim, Dad would fire up the old Massey-Ferguson and head into the storage area of the building that housed the cider press. There was a large cold room, big enough to roller skate and ride bikes in, a sorting conveyor belt that separated the apples according to size, and a boxing area for preparing apples for shipping to markets. Any apples that were not pretty enough for fresh sales were considered perfect for cider and would make their way to the press room. I have no idea how old the press was, but it was one impressive piece of machinery. It took up the whole upper room of the press barn and was made up of a series of burlap and muslin sheets stretched tight, levers, pulleys, spigots, spouts, and what looked like hardwood cutting boards that did the actual pressing. The apples went in whole and were crushed by the sheer power of the press. The fresh cider would come out through a hose, go directly into cider bottles, and be capped and put in the cooler within moments. The pulp that remained was as dry as flour, not a bit of moisture was left in the pressed apples. We fed the apple pulp to our milk cows and Dad claimed it made the milk sweeter.

I've always thought it interesting that something as wonderful as an apple has to be utterly destroyed to make something as wonderful as apple cider. The same thing happens to grapes for wine, peaches for homemade jam, or the dismantling of a crumbling barn to create the barn wood furniture that William makes in his wood shop. Something good is always sacrificed when something else is made. The

beauty of a pasture must give way to the beauty of tilled soil if a harvest is to be had. The beauty of a tree must give way to the beauty of craftsmanship if a home is to be built. The beauty of youth must give way to age if a life is to be lived fully.

It's part of the natural cycle of things. Life is like a cider press at points of growth. It presses down against us, squeezing us with anxiety, fear, stress, and pain until we think we can bear no more; and when the pressure eases, we find that if we have borne it well, we are a new creation. An apple is not apple cider, but the potential for cider was in the apple all along. We are not perfect, but the potential for perfection is within us. Not necessarily perfect beauty, perfect fitness, or perfect knowledge, but the ability to act in perfect kindness, with perfect love and compassion. It takes being pressed to the point of being crushed ourselves to appreciate the amount of compassion others need from us.

Our cider could not have been made without the cushion of the burlap to hold the apples while they suffered. It may have been course, unrefined, and imperfect, but it was strong and it held true when the press began its work. Our cider would not have been ready for the bottles without the muslin, its fine weave and simple purity strained out the last of the pulp that could lead to decay within the bottles.

How often in our lives does an unrefined, imperfect person hold us up and support us when we think we'll be crushed? We may flail against them, hate them for holding us, or wish we could get away from their restraints, but there is no escaping the trials of living life without denying ourselves the blessings of it also. We can only hope there is someone who can help us through. How often does some simple, unadorned friend help us to strain out the things in our life that would destroy us? We may not want to give up the last pieces of who we were, but how can we become a new creation if we are unwilling to let go of what held us back in the first place?

We sacrificed our apples to make our apple cider. We gave up the volume of solid fruit for the smaller, but sweeter, amount of juice that was prized and of greater value. What do we have in our own lives that resemble apple cider? What is it that we are holding onto that is holding us back from becoming what we most want to be? Do we hold onto fear when we want to take a new path? My brother started medical school with a wife and six kids in tow. He had eight before he finished. I imagine he and my sister-in-law went through a multitude of apple press moments before they made it out the other side of schooling and the fear it can engender. But at this point they wouldn't trade any of it. They are where they want to be, helping people, thriving in a small mid-Western town where they can live, work, and serve among the people they love. My Dad lost his wife and a daughter on a foggy Christmas day over forty years ago. He bought two graves and the doctor told him to buy three more for his other children who he didn't think would pull through. I imagine the sorrow and fear of those days pressed against him, and he felt at times that he would be crushed. But there were hands that reached out to help hold him in place while all he could do was bear the pain of change and help his children bear it too. My brother Jared once asked him, "How did you survive it Dad?" He thought about it for a moment and he said, "I had a family who needed me. I had to survive it." From that crushing loss came the comfort of my Mom and the addition of five more children that now make up our family.

> Change is inevitable.
> It is up to us to determine
> if the change is beautiful or not.
> Crushed apples can be made into apple cider
> or vinegar depending on the care taken
> with the results of the crushing.

Change is inevitable. It is up to us to determine if the change is beautiful or not. Crushed apples can be made into apple cider or vinegar depending on the care taken with the results of the crushing. Tilled soil can become a bed of weeds without care and commitment; old barn wood can just rot away to nothing if it isn't reformed into a work of art.

When you find yourself in the cider press, when you fear being crushed and losing yourself in the process, remember: you are not your trials, you are the strength the trials show; you are not your disappointments, you are the hope that overcomes loss; you are not your disabilities, you are your thoughts, your dreams, and your knowledge which knows no disadvantage or restraints; you are not your sorrow, sorrow is a part of what makes you human, capable of compassion, generosity, and love; you are not your fears, fear is the lie that tries to hide your faith. Choose faith. Your choices will determine your outcome. Choose well that your life may be sweeter, stronger, and a reminder to everyone you have the opportunity to serve that there is always hope, strength, faith, and love available for those that hold on and allow themselves to be held.

Little Ethel

A Christmas Story of Faith and Family

Principle #6: The love that binds a family, the love that has the power to bind the world, is eternal

November 2006

　　I saw it while I was rummaging through my mother's pictures. She has so many that I believe I was meant to find it, to remember my childhood and be reminded of a time long before I was born; before my mother was born; when the woman I called Grandma was a small girl. It's such a small thing really to have had such an impact on my life, and I don't believe I fully understood what that impact was until I held that tiny three by five-inch photo in my hand and stared into the face of a child I had heard of in a story from the time I was old enough to crawl into my Grandma's lap.

　　It was my favorite story.

　　It's odd that it should have been my favorite story, odder yet that my Grandma would have told it to me in the first place. It's the kind of story I would tell my own children in order to warn them of dangers and to remind them of things they shouldn't do. But Grandma told it, and I remember every word.

December 1978

"It's so deep." With my nose pushed in like a Boston terrier's against the picture window in the dining room, I stated the obvious in the way that young children often do. The snow was deep, three feet at the last measuring and still falling. Snow wasn't unusual. We lived high in the Cascade Mountains of Northern California, outside the small town of Montgomery Creek, and it always snowed; most of the time I thought of it as a marvelous thing. It was deep enough to tunnel through and build forts, endless mountains of it. Of course, all of that snow meant that my father also had to tunnel from the house to the barn in order to milk the cows and tunnel from the house to the car and from the car to the driveway and from the driveway, which was very steep, all the way to the road so that we could make our way to the grocery store or to church. But in my own insular little world I only saw beautiful snow as I sat by the huge window, sipping hot apple cider made from our own apples and waiting.

It was two days before Christmas, and they were due to arrive any minute. We knew they were coming. They had never not been there for Christmas, and they were as constant as the sunrise. It would be hard to see them because of all the white snow; their old car, lovingly called "The White Hornet," would blend into the scenery and we would only be able to see them by their headlights.

"Here comes the White Hornet!" my Dad would call, and we, my brothers and I, would press up against the window calling, "Where? Where?"

Then my mother, whose sweet soul couldn't stand to see us disappointed, would say, "Don't tease them." And then turn to us and say, "They'll be here soon, don't worry." It was all part of the fun, Dad's teasing, and Mom's comforting. It added to the anticipation, to the joy at their arrival.

Finally, when the day and my mother's nerves had worn on, we would see their lights round the last turn on Old Cove Road, and pandemonium would ensue. For all of our waiting and watching, we were never ready to rush out and

greet them. We would have to rush first for coats, hats, mittens, and boots. When we were as wide with wraps as the snow was deep, we would run out the door and trip over each other on the way to their car.

And there they were, the two most beautiful people in my world: Grandma and Grandpa Stratton.

Grandma would hop out of the car with her arms spread wide and gather all of us up in a hug. She always smelled so good. Her bright red hair would be tied up with a piece of wrapping yarn, red because it was almost Christmas, and she would be wearing the cream sweater with the green zigzags. Her smile and kisses were warm and sweet. She was perfect. She always sat in the passenger seat because she never learned to drive a car. My Mom said once that Grandma never learned because Grandpa didn't have the patience to teach her, which is probably true. But I think Grandma was content to be a passenger and sit back and enjoy the journey; it was just as much fun to go somewhere as it was to finally get there. Wherever she went she would look everywhere and drink in the views. She could tell you in detail about all of the things she had seen; she was a first rate observer.

On the far side of the car, just putting his canes out and pushing himself up was the man I loved as much as I loved my Dad. Grandpa would raise one of his hands as he leaned against the car and call out a greeting, his smile so full of love and pride that I can remember the glow of that feeling still today. He was always so proud of the children we were and the people we were growing into, and we knew it. I didn't realize at the time how lucky I was to have someone love me that much.

Hugs would be shared all the way around, Grandma and Grandpa, Mom and Dad, Kirk, Kris, Aaron, Jared, and I. Everybody had to get their fill of hugs before we could unload. I'm still amazed at how much stuff could fit in the back of that little car. We never doubted that there was a Santa at our

house. He arrived every year with the White Hornet. It was an unspoken rule that we weren't really supposed to count the presents and compare who had the most, but I always did it anyway. There are benefits to being the baby in a big family; I usually had a lot of presents. We would pack in the presents and pile them under the tree, and they would spill out at least five feet onto the rug around its base.

I lived in a Christmas card setting, high mountains, snow, a huge light-covered Christmas tree, and enough presents to rival Toyland. Now, we had a lot of presents, but they weren't all from a store; in fact, I would say most of them weren't. We used to wrap our own toys and give them to each other just because it was so fun to see something wrapped. Every year the local school held a "Santa's Workshop" for the children in the area. Everyone in the community donated items, and then the children could go in and choose one gift for each member of their family. The gift would cost only 10¢ and that was only to cover the cost of the wrapping paper.

I remember seeing my brother come out with a pair of old beat-up roller skates. The rubber wheels were gone, so all that was left was the metal. I was so excited to get those skates I couldn't stand it. It didn't matter that they were going to shake the teeth out of my head if I tried to actually skate on them; they were from my brother. My Mom still has this horrible old fruit bowl that one of my brothers picked out for her at the workshop. I don't think she'd trade it for all the crystal in Tiffany's. It sits in a place of honor on her kitchen counter top, always full of bananas or apples.

After the presents were brought in from the Hornet, the suitcases had to be unloaded. Grandma supported every cliché about women when it came to packing. I don't know why she had to pack ten different outfits for their stay at our house because if memory serves, she wore the same thing most of the time. I guess she wanted to be prepared. She would always bring her own pillow too. It had a satin pillowcase, and I just knew that it was the kind of pillowcase

that a princess would use. Then there was the makeup case. It was a fascinating mystery—creams, powders, lotions, and perfumes. She would open the lid and it smelled like bottled Grandma. I wish I could find an air freshener that smelled as good as that did to me.

Yes, Grandma's cases were amazing and fantastic, but the true wonder was Grandpa's medicine case.

Grandpa was taking vitamins and minerals before it became the popular thing to do. He was taking zinc, B12, and magnesium every day when the doctors were still saying that it didn't do you any good to take vitamin pills. He may have lost the full use of his legs, but the rest of his body was as healthy as a horse. He even had a mortar and pestle. I would watch him grind up all of the vitamins that had been so carefully pressed into nice little pills, mix the dust with his Metamucil and drink it all down like it was lemonade. It disgusted and fascinated me at the same time.

They would bring persimmons with them; I never ate them as a child because they looked a little too slimy. I eat them now and enjoy them as I remember my Mom and Grandma would. They would sit at the table, eating persimmons, drinking rose-hip tea, and catching up on all of the latest news. We would hear about Paul and Marla, about Whitney and Bernice, about Grandma's sisters, and Grandpa's family. I didn't know half of the people, but I would sit with them and imagine that I was a grown-up lady visiting and sharing all the news. Without fail my mother would say "So, tell me what else" during the course of the conversation. It has become my Mom's signature statement. One of my niece's when she was about two years old, when asked "What does Grandma say?" would answer "So what else." My Mom is a conversation connoisseur.

The evening meal would be a joyous time. It seems that every meal at our house was a joyous time. It wasn't because of the food we ate though my mom is a fantastic

cook; it was simply the joy of being together. Meals were filled with laughter, stories, full stomachs, and full hearts.

When all traces of the meal had been cleaned, we would sit in the glow of the Christmas tree lights. I'm sure that there must have been talk of Christmases past and hopes for the future, but I don't remember much besides the tree and the lights. The tree was acquired by means of a lengthy tradition. On the day after Thanksgiving, or shortly thereafter, we would all trudge through the snow out to the truck and pile in. We would drive for what seemed a long time (mostly because there were usually six people piled into the truck, and going any distance with that many people in such a small space seems to last a long time) and then stop beneath a forest of huge pine trees. Out we would fall and begin our trek through more snow. My Mom has amazing taste in Christmas trees. She can spot the perfect tree at 100 yards, but she doubts her own ability. Because of this doubt Mom would usually find "the tree" within the first ten minutes of the yearly tree hunt, and we would then spend another two hours tramping through the snow looking at every tree in the forest "just in case" we might have missed one that was better. We invariably returned to the first tree. She carries this ability into the realm of shopping. She can find the perfect gift within ten minutes too, but she has to see everything in the store and the warehouse in the back just to cover all of her bases.

After the tree was picked out, with Dad shaking his head and Kris muttering, the cutting down would commence. We had a large room and Mom wanted a big enough tree to fill the space, so Kris would scale up into the tree to cut it down and Mom would keep saying "Don't cut it too short! Make it just a little taller!" When it was finally down it would be twenty feet tall and would have filled our barn. So home we'd go where Kris would trim off about twelve feet of tree; and up it would go. The lights would go on first and then the ornaments would come out. My Mom never picked themes for the house and tree like people do these days. Instead the tree would be covered with memories. As each ornament

came out of the box she would tell us it's story, whether it was from her childhood or from last year's kindergarten class.

I helped her hang many of those ornaments just a couple of years ago, and she told the same stories. I could tell a few of them, and we wept together for the joy of the memories and the sorrow that those who gave them to us are gone now. When it was completed, it was a masterpiece, glittering and bright. I could sit for hours watching the lights and hearing the softly scratchy sound of Christmas songs on the record player. The Walton family would be singing "Hark! The Herald Angels Sing!" while I snuggled next to Grandma on the couch and felt that everything was perfect. It's amazing to look back at the child I was and realize how precious it was to feel so full of joy from having a full tummy, warm toes, and a room full of family. I forget sometimes as I get older just how precious those things really are.

Just when I was sleepy enough to start nodding off against Grandma's shoulder, we would retire to our room for the night. Grandpa would get to sleep in my bed, Grandma and I would stay in my brothers' bed, and to this day I have no idea where my brothers slept. All I knew was that I got to share with Grandma. She would change into her nightgown, use some of the magic potions from her makeup case, then lay in the very center of the bed, propped up on her satin pillow. Aaron, Jared, and I would all climb up onto the bed with her, waiting impatiently for bedtime stories to begin. Without fail she would ask "What story do you want to hear?" and our answer was always the same, "Little Ethel, tell us about Little Ethel!" She would laugh in a perplexed sort of way and say, almost to herself, "Why do you always want to hear about Little Ethel?" But we never doubted that she would tell us.

Summer 1921

"In those days" Grandma would begin, "we didn't travel by cars; we had to ride in a wagon. So your great-grandpa, my Daddy, would hook up the team and we would drive to our cousin's home. It took a long time to get there so

when we went, we stayed for several days. There were lots of grown-ups and even more children, and we all liked to play together. Now Little Ethel (here she would pause and explain that Little Ethel was called Little Ethel because her Mother was called Big Ethel) and her brother had a ball that all of the cousins loved to play catch with. So after supper the children were sent to play in the field beyond the barn. It was lots of fun with the children running here and there in the field and around some large bales of cotton that had been harvested earlier in the year. One of the older cousins threw the ball and it fell beyond where the children could reach it. So Little Ethel climbed up on top of the cotton bales and made her way to where the ball had fallen into one of the open bales. It was evening, and beginning to get cool and when it gets cool the snakes try to find places that are warm to stay for the night, but Little Ethel couldn't see that a cotton mouth snake was coiled up inside the warm cotton. All that she could see was her ball and so she reached her little arm down to get it and when she almost had it, the snake struck and bit her on the wrist."

Grandma always paused here and would show us on her own wrist just where Little Ethel had been bitten. I can remember picturing myself as that long ago little girl being shocked at the pain of a snake bite. "We all screamed for the adults, and Little Ethel's father came running and scooped her up while one of the men hooked up the horses and wagon to

take her to the nearest doctor. Her father drove the team as fast as he could while Little Ethel's mother held her in the back, but the trip to the doctor's took over an hour and by the time they reached him it was too late to save her and she died."

Christmas 1978

That was the end of the story, Grandma never elaborated on what happened after Little Ethel died. She would go on to stories about Toyland and fairy tales, and I don't think I ever thought any more that Christmas about the little girl who died 50 years before I was born.

Christmas morning would arrive, with all of the excitement you would expect, but none of the chaos. My Mom insisted that we eat breakfast before presents, and when we were through the presents would be handed out one by one and would be opened in the same way. That way the joy of giving as well as receiving could be shared with the whole family. It seemed to last forever, it was so wonderful to be sitting there amidst wrapping paper and bows and all the treasures that Santa had brought.

I don't ever remember feeling the "after-Christmas letdown" that people talk about. For me the whole day was wonderful, the days that followed were just as wonderful. Grandma would walk with us to the top of the driveway and exclaim over the view of the barnyard just as she would if we walked a half-mile further and could see the entire Mt. Shasta valley. She saw beauty and joy in things that others would have passed by. We were sad when they finally climbed into the White Hornet and drove away. We would wave until they made the last turn far up the hillside and we knew they couldn't see us anymore. We would miss them, but it was part of the experience; the joy of their arrival, the sadness of their departure, and the knowing that we would see them again soon.

November 2006

So I sit here tonight, staring at this small picture that has started my reminiscing. A little dark-haired girl stands beside her brother on a flower-framed porch. A sweet smile is on her face and in her eyes, while her brother grins with the exuberance of boyhood. Her little hand rests on his head in a gesture so natural and comfortable that I don't imagine it was contrived for the photograph.

It makes me sad. I think of how short her life was, perhaps only two years past when this image was taken and I can't help but wonder how her short life and tragic death touched those around her.

What happened to that grinning young boy who seemed to love his little sister so much? I never thought of it as a child, but now that I have children of my own I wonder at what an agony it would have been for her mother and father to drive to the doctor's with such fear and hope only to return home again with such pain and loss. I wonder if Ethel rocked her baby girl on the trip home from the doctor's and wept over her lifeless form. It breaks my heart to think of it. I think of the family waiting at home, the young cousins anxious to hear news of their playmate. I think of my Grandma. She was just a little girl herself, only five or six at the time. I don't know how the death of that child affected the others, but I can see what influence it had on my Grandma and on my mother and on me.

Grandma knew what loss was. She understood that life was neither fair nor easy, but she never let that destroy her optimism. Life is hard? Yes, but life is also beautiful. Life ends? Yes, but life also goes on.

I believe that Grandma learned at an early age to never take beauty and joy for granted. Perfection isn't a place you get to and start setting up house; it's found in countless tiny moments every day that God grants you the gift of breath. Joy is in the way the sunlight hits the clouds after a rainstorm. Perfection is in the way the wind throws the leaves across your path as you walk home from the grocery store. Beauty is in the smile of the young woman you complimented on the way home from work. And most of all I believe that Grandma learned that the deepest heartache and the truest joy is found within our own families. She never let an opportunity to say "I love you" pass her by because she never knew when the opportunity to say it would come again.

> Perfection isn't a place you get to and start setting up house; it's found in countless tiny moments every day that God grants you the gift of breath.

I think the loss of a childhood friend affected Grandma in countless ways and helped to make of her the woman she became. Because of the woman she was, my own mother learned to be generous with her time and talents—to go the extra mile because it never hurts to make sure that everything is just as it should be, not just with trees and gifts, but with hearts and homes. Mom always has a smile and a kind word; she never lets an opportunity to say something kind get by her. Life is too short to spend it with a frown on your face so she smiles wherever she goes—not because she has never known sadness or disappointment but because she chooses to see that there is more to life than that.

Joy is a gift that flows from God; you have only to open your heart to it.

It hurts, because along with the joy is the knowledge that it comes with a price. My grandmother and my mother like our great mother Eve before us understood that the price for joy is sorrow, but it is worth the cost. Would Ethel have

traded one beat of Little Ethel's heart if she had known there would be so few? I don't think so. Did she regret having had a child just because she lost her so soon? How can you regret beauty or malign joy?

Christmas is nearly here, and there is a stirring in my heart for the souls that have come before me. I see this little girl and it occurs to me that she will never be forgotten so long as I remember her and tell her story. My grandmother will live on because I have taught my children about who she was. My mom will be forever treasured in the hearts of her children and grandchildren. And beyond all of us, there is a voice that whispers to my heart and tells me that there was another life, in another time, full of joy and sorrow, beauty and perfection that made all that I feel possible. If my heart breaks at the pain of a mother's loss, He takes my broken heart and heals it with the Father's gift of faith. I think of all that the Savior's life teaches about finding joy in small things, about looking past pain to choose the better part of faith. My family has taught me that, not just in words, but in every deed.

Grandma and Grandpa are gone now. Little Ethel and her mother and father are no longer separated by death, but rather joined by it. I miss them. Some I never knew, and some I loved as much as it is possible to love. This gratitude for a family who cherishes the good and forgives the bad, who looks for the joy and endures the sorrow fills my soul.

I long to see those whom I have loved and lost long since. I wish to tell them of the legacy of faith and family that I will pass on because of the lives they lived. But for now I am content to be as I was as a child watching the White Hornet pull out of sight on a winding mountain road. I know that I can't see them anymore, but I know that I will see them again soon and until that day I will treasure every moment I have here.

I will open my heart to the joy that God has in abundance for those who desire it. Because isn't that what the Christmas story truly tells? To learn to bow to the will of God,

no matter how difficult, and to find that there is peace in the midst of trials, and help when the night seems darkest. If the glory of God could reside in such a humble place as a stable, then why could joy not rest in my own home? I will seek it every day, glean it from the enthusiasm of my children, gather it in their laughter, and treasure it in my heart for all eternity.

Toboggan Hill

Principle #7: Learn to recognize your seasons

I grew up on the side of a mountain, well several mountains really, all of which were located in Northern California. We prided ourselves on living in the shadow of two volcanoes, Mt. Shasta and Mt. Lassen, without fear. When we first moved to the Midwest I used to find great delight in telling people, "Yeah, I grew up with a volcano in my backyard." It wasn't strictly true, it was more like an hour away, but I really did enjoy the resulting big-eyed stare and the question, "Weren't you terrified? How could you stand the earthquakes?" I never actually felt an earthquake while growing up in California so instead I would try to sound very nonchalant. "Oh, most earthquakes are only a 3.5 or so, you don't even feel those." Eventually I tired of the fabricated closeness to geological danger and tried in vain to explain that I grew up in Northern California which was a long ways from palm treed beaches, earthquakes, and a good tan—that it was in fact more like their own farming town. They didn't like the truth so we stopped discussing it altogether.

People usually love what they grow up with if they have happy memories to associate with it. I have a multitude of happy memories surrounding the mountains: watching Kirk and Kris fish in icy cold mountain streams for trout; seeing the fat snowflakes turn steadily into deep drifts and the pine trees to silent white sentinels of winter; listening to the gentle hum of bees over the wildflowers in the high meadows; the sound of the evening winds whispering through pine boughs; the

crisp, clean smell of morning on a cold fall day, the spice of apples and fallen leaves undertones to the newly distilled rain; the warm musky smell of wood smoke rising and drifting with the wind, and the Toboggan Hill.

Toboggan Hill climbed up from the little used road that ran from the barn through the field to the hog shed and boasted at its top a large pine tree which was perfect for climbing. We loved to climb trees, my brothers and I. We had favorite climbing pines all over the farm. The one beside the chicken coop was another favorite, mostly because that one was off-limits. Toboggan Hill was also the perfect spot to rest in the summer and it was the beginning of a sled track that we would fly down every winter.

It was a good hill, steep enough to provide sufficient speed to be fun (because who wants to sled down a hill slowly?) without being so steep that you felt like a kamikaze pilot headed for the last showdown. There were a few minor bumps on the hill that added variation to the ride depending on which fork you took, left, right, or straight down the middle, but all tracks led to the same ending: the road.

But, and there always has to be a "but", there was one large problem at the bottom of the hill and on the other side of the road: blackberry bushes. Anyone who has lived in the Northwest can attest to the fact that wild blackberry bushes are the bane of every farmer. They multiply like rabbits on fertility medication; they take over pastures, bury fences, cover buildings, and in our case provided a challenge to snow bound children.

Here is how a good run down Toboggan Hill would work: At the top of the hill a group of between 3 to 7 children and teenagers would gather under the pine tree and argue, debate, and fight over who would go down first. Once that dilemma was over the order in which they sat on the toboggan was hotly debated. It was generally agreed that the smallest member of the expedition (which was always me) would sit in the back so as to avoid any injuries and recriminations from

Mom later. Other than that it was just a matter of who climbed on fastest and held on tightest to their position. If the person in front was a good driver and could avoid being shoved by the rest of the group, he or she could lead the group down the hill, all whooping and hollering gleefully and turn the toboggan successfully onto the road at the bottom of the hill without crossing it fully and landing everyone in the blackberry bushes on the other side.

This feat was harder to accomplish than it sounds. I myself was never the driver of the Johnson Toboggan Train; I was usually flying off the back of it when we hit the first bump. But it was winter and we had enough layers of clothing on to keep us well protected from the cold and any possible bruising caused by bouncing down the hillside. Turning a six-foot toboggan is hard with one rider, turning a 6-foot toboggan with 4 or 5 riders is almost impossible but they were up to the challenge.

Here is how a bad run down toboggan hill would work: Take everything from the previous description up until the whooping and hollering gleefully and then fail to turn the toboggan successfully. Usually one of two things would happen. Either the toboggan would turn "almost" far enough but not quite and everyone would be tossed off the side and into the brambles, or they wouldn't get it turned at all and they would crash head on into the thorns that clung like talons and claws.

The thrill of the ride was enough to keep us trudging back up the hill every time, even when we were picking thorns out of our snow pants, but what really kept us going back time and again was what would happen if we made a superior run down Toboggan Hill.

There was one spot in the mass of blackberry brambles that was a little lower than the rest. If whoever was driving could manage to steer the sled into that narrow opening the toboggan and all its riders would sail right over the tangled vines and continue even further down the hill

finally coming to rest in the pasture. It made the ride twice as long and the satisfaction of having beaten the berries was off the charts.

Needless to say there were many attempts to accomplish a superior run and multiple failures resulting in an increase of bad runs, an occasional swear word, and several obligatory snowball fights. But it was worth it. It was worth the threat of thorns in our pants to keep going a little further, a little faster, to sail a little higher over the barrier in our road.

It's interesting how a little snow can change your perspective. During the summer months those berry vines were a nuisance, but we could avoid them. It wasn't difficult to skirt them on the road or walk around them in the field. We never considered tackling the berries in a toboggan any other time of year. Why would we? But during the winter months when we couldn't skirt them, when the drifted snow made it impossible to avoid them, we willingly faced them head on.

> There is a rhythm and cycle
> to a life lived close to nature
> that allows you
> to know which season
> is best for each endeavor you pursue.

Difficulties can do that to you. They soften the edges, like snow. And sometimes they harden and shatter a person's spirit like ice. It's all in how you face it.

The more we raced down Toboggan Hill and faced the stickers and thorns the wider and easier the path became on each successive run. Sometimes we missed and landed in a scratched-up heap, but we got back up and tried again. And sometimes we didn't try at all and the more we turned into the road the harder and more packed the ice and snow by the berries became, blocking our way and tugging at our sled when we tried to turn it into a different path.

76

I don't think we were any braver in winter than in summer. It wasn't a matter of bravery at all that led us to try to conquer our thorns; it was simply knowing our seasons.

There is a rhythm and cycle to a life lived close to nature that allows you to know which season is best for each endeavor you pursue. We don't plant corn in winter; not because we don't like corn and not because planting corn isn't a worthy and noble activity. Very simply: corn won't grow in the winter. It doesn't matter how often you try to plant it in the snow, it simply will not sprout. Likewise we never try to toboggan over the berries in the spring and summer. There's nothing to help lift us over them when it's warm and we may destroy the fruit on them. It's just wiser to make the attempt when we know we have a chance to accomplish our goal.

Since leaving Hillcrest Orchards I've tried to race down several toboggan runs in the wrong season, not recognizing beforehand that I was ill-equipped to make it across the challenge I'd given myself. I really believe that we are capable of facing challenges and overcoming them, but sometimes it isn't a matter of bravery or belief or dedication. Sometimes it is simply the wrong season. And when our season to sail over the challenge arrives, if we take a run at it again and again and again we'll find that we will indeed make it past the thorns and vines that stand in our way.

Patrick's Point

Principle #8: Compassion is a way of life; offer it to all living things

Hillcrest Orchards was in the Cascade Mountains about two hours northeast of Redding, California, and a little over three hours from the Northern California coast. I used to laugh when we moved to Missouri and people would invariably make "California Girl" remarks. I had to explain that the northern coast was nothing like the sunny, southern California beaches. I didn't surf, sunbathe, or go bikini clad on the beaches I frequented. I was more likely to be swathed in a sweater, jacket, and ball cap to keep off the rain. I loved the rough, wild and untamed temperament of the rocky, northern strand. I loved the crash and bellow of the wind and the waves. I used to sit for what seemed hours and just bask in the way the Earth trembled in response to the sea. It was primal, elemental, and invigorating to feel the power of it around me.

We went once a year, almost every year, in November for my Dad's birthday. It was a family tradition. Mom would throw 50 pounds of potatoes in the back of the old truck, 5 dozen eggs, and 10 loaves of bread, along with some bacon and sausage from a pig we'd butchered earlier in the fall and hot cocoa mix, graham crackers, Hershey's chocolate bars, and Stay-Puft marshmallows from a store on the way over to the coast. I know that sounds like a lot of food, but remember that we had a lot of kids to feed. We'd then drive, packed into the truck like a bunch of canned sardines, through the

mountains down to Redding, past Whiskeytown Lake, Whiskeytown itself (before it was refurbished into a tourist attraction), and over the coastal mountains to the little town of Trinidad on the coast and on up the road to Patrick's Point State Park.

It was a beautiful park, situated directly on the coast and incorporating wooded trails, whale watching promontories, and sea surrounded boulders that could be accessed by trails and bridges. We loved to climb Wedding Rock, past the safety rails to sit and dangle our feet over the wave-tumbled rocks some 30 feet below us. We hiked down to Agate Beach where we would scour the ground for the brightly colored, sea smoothed rocks that it was named for. We filled our pockets with the amber, green, blue, and pink stones, and weeks later when we were back on the farm, roasting ourselves by the wood stove trying to stay warm, we'd find them in the crevices of those pockets, the last pebbles that remained after washing and line drying. We'd pull them out and they'd smell ever so slightly of the sea, a reminder of the fun and frolic of our ocean adventures.

Dad always tried to find a campsite that didn't have a ton of people around, and since it was November that wasn't too difficult. We were almost always the only ones out there; it was like having the whole park to ourselves. Dad backed into the parking space and we'd pile out of the truck, a little drunk from gas fumes and begin camp set up. Grandpa Stratton had found a huge, old, broken-down picnic basket at the local Salvation Army store and had done a fine job of patching it up. It became our camping basket, always full of mismatched dishes, silverware, cooking utensils, and Mom's gigantic cast-iron skillet that smelled of campfires. The park boasted stone fireplaces built by the Civilian Conservation Corp during the great depression and wooden camp pantries where dry goods could be housed and kept safe from the rain. Occasionally when you'd pull into camp, there would be a sign on the Rangers' office that said "Bear in camp: DO NOT leave food out." If that was the case we didn't use the pantry, we left the food in the truck. We had an old army tent that

sometimes we used and sometimes we didn't. It was something of an ordeal to set it up, and I gladly avoided it and offered to help Mom instead. I helped her arrange bread, some peanut butter and homemade blackberry jam, spices, cocoa, and S'mores ingredients in the pantry and then wandered the campsite to glean any deadfall for the fire. As a general rule we brought our own firewood, the wood at the coast is continually wet, but we tried to keep the campsite tidy by burning anything that was tinder or kindling size. It was a good job for a little girl, it kept me out of trouble and out from underfoot. As soon as the tent was up, sleeping spots claimed and cooking supplies set out for Mom we would race off, Kris in the lead, for Agate Beach and any tide pools left to play in.

The descent to the beach wound its way down a steep cliff path. The taller members of our troop could see over the windswept shrubs that grew all over it but since I was short the thing that fascinated me most was the world that existed under the shrubbery. We called it "Middle Earth" and I imagined us on a great quest to find where the White Ships were sailing from. I hadn't read Tolkien's works at that tender age. I was ten before I reached for our copy of The Hobbit, but I knew the story somehow and I was eager to play a part in a noble adventure. I would climb beneath the leggy branches of the sea-stunted trees and race my brothers down the side of the mountain to the shore. Every time we visited Patrick's Point the bottom of the trail to the beach would be in a different place or in varying stages of disrepair. The rangers fought a continual battle with the waves to keep the beach accessible.

When we reached the edge of civilization and the Pacific raged in front of us, stretching all the way to China, I'd morph from "Middle Earth adventurer" to "Scientific Explorer," out to discover a new form of life along the seashore. In the tide pools we'd find hermit crabs, small, transparent jellyfish looking animals that I have no other name for, and occasionally starfish and sea urchins. I knew in my heart I'd never make it as a scientist. I was grossed out by the thought of actually holding one of those animals. I loved to

look at them, to observe their colors, shapes, and textures, but touch them? No thanks. I left that to Aaron and Jared.

We loved the bulbous, onion looking bladders of the seaweed also. We could never tell which part was the top and which was the bottom. It was unlike any plant that grew on the farm and it never made any sense to me, but it made a wonderful weapon to throw at brothers when we dug foxholes on the beach and reenacted D-Day. As long as the sunlight, filtered as it was by clouds, would hold out we'd play in the waves, the wind, and the sand. I'm sure we were cold and shivery, but it just served to make the play more real. Hunger would drive us back up the hill to the campfire where Mom would have already made a wonderful dinner of homemade "hash" which was just cubed potatoes, sausage, onions, and spices. Occasionally we'd dress it up with cheese or eggs but, however we ate them they were wonderful. I still feel nostalgic whenever I eat potatoes.

We prayed over our meal, a ritual that we followed no matter where we were, and then tucked in like a starving mob. We sat around the campfire visiting until the logs burned down to embers. We'd make S'mores and debate the value of a nicely toasted marshmallow versus a charbroiled black one while the firelight died down to a gentle glow. I would sit on a make-shift log chair, wrapped up in a camp blanket, watching the coals burn themselves down to ashes while the soft hum of conversation filled the cozy air around us. Finally, when my eyes wouldn't stay open any longer someone would shoo me off to bed. I'd crawl into a sleeping bag, tuck an old flattened camp pillow under my head, and dream of crashing waves and barking sea lions waiting to greet me in the morning from the tide drenched rocks near the shore.

There was one particular trip to the ocean which I remember to this day. We had followed all of our family camp rituals: tent, organizing, beach run, dinner, etc. and had slept soundly through the night, but when we awoke in the morning we discovered that Mom's camp pantry had been broken into.

We puzzled over it all morning. There were no bear signs at the Rangers office and no physical signs of them either. The lock had been turned, the door opened and Mom's cooking supplies rifled through very neatly. We were of course interrogated, but I don't think any of us would have ever considered stealing the cooking supplies. Why would we? We were going to eat it all anyway, and it tasted better when Mom made it than when we did. Mom thought that either one of us was sleeping walking (which wasn't unheard of at our house) or someone had gotten into our supplies.

We played all day, watched for whales to glide by, which they never did because it was so late in the year, and settled in again for our second night at camp.

Once again in the morning we discovered that we had been robbed. The peanut butter lid was on the table but the jar was gone.

"Who takes a jar of peanut butter without the lid?" Mom asked the universe at large. We were all stumped, and grateful that at least the thief hadn't made off with the potatoes and bacon which would have cut the trip woefully short.

We ran up and down the rocks and beaches again that day. We watched the sea lions cavorting on their rocks and in the waves and listened to them bark at us while we whooped and hollered. It was our last full day at the coast and we made the most of it.

That night, after hash, S'mores, cocoa and stories told around the campfire my Mom decided to lay a trap for the camp thief. She was determined to find out who the culprit was. She made herself a bed on the tailgate of the old pickup, her flashlight in hand and waited.

The embers burned low to just a hint of light, the sea breezes blew clouds past the crisp, clear fall stars as it grew later and later and still no thief appeared. Finally, as the night grew darker around her, Mom heard a rustle in the leaves at

the edge of the campsite. She breathed shallowly, waiting for the culprit to come further in before she revealed who it was. She could hear more rustling sounds, a scuffling of sorts, and the distinct "click" as the pantry latch was turned and the door swung open.

Mom jumped into action; she flipped the flashlight's switch, shone it on the pantry, and stared at a scraggly raccoon standing on its back legs, paws in the pantry, just grabbing our last loaf of bread. It was as startled as Mom was, but recovered faster, hissing and running off, bread in tow into the underbrush.

> When kindness is the way you live your life,
>
> choosing to be kind is easier,
>
> wanting to share
>
> with even the meanest of animals
>
> becomes second nature,
>
> and your ability to feel joy increases.

Well Mom wasn't having any of that, she'd been stolen from enough so she took off through the ferns and downed limbs chasing the raccoon into the forest. It was easy enough to tail the raccoon since she was having trouble moving quickly what with a full loaf of bread clamped between her teeth. Mom almost caught up with her a couple of times, but the raccoon would dodge and keep going. She was just as determined to keep her booty as Mom was to reclaim it. Finally the raccoon reached the base of an old tree, where she backed into a hollowed out spot by the roots and snarled at Mom again, her paws clutching the bread desperately. Mom ignored the hissing and shone the beam from the flashlight into the recesses of the tree roots. A handful of tiny eyes gleamed back at her, and slowly a group of five or six scrawny baby raccoons came climbing out to cling to their mothers back while she took her stand over a morsel of bread for their dinner.

Mom shined the light back on the mother raccoon and looked at her, sides heaving from running with the treasure of her nightly raid, eyes fierce with a desire to protect her young

and her own body thin and hungry. Mom just sighed and said, "Go ahead and keep it girl. Feed your family," and walked alone and empty-handed back to our campsite.

Mom told us in the morning who our thief had been. She said, "I felt so bad for her. She looked so thin and hungry. I just couldn't take the bread back from her." We ate potatoes again instead of French toast, but none of us were sorry. And none of us were surprised. Mom has a gentle and generous heart, capable of a giving that I have never seen an equal to. The only thing that rivals her generosity of spirit is her vigilant defense of those she calls her family. I think she saw a kindred spirit in that care-worn raccoon that night, another mother who was desperate to take care of her family. She had known what it felt like to be alone and responsible for the care and health of a young brood. She had escaped her abusive first marriage and been the sole provider for her two young sons. She had worked two jobs just to keep them in a home and fed. She knew what it was to struggle against fear, loneliness, and desperation. And she knew how much it meant to experience a touch of kindness now and then in the midst of her trials. So she let the raccoon have the bread. It was just a small thing, inconsequential one might say. But Mom's life has been made up of a long string of what she'd call "inconsequential" kindnesses that have had lasting, eternal consequences for good.

Abraham Lincoln once said, "I care not for a man's religion whose dog and cat are not the better for it." I can say from having known her for a lifetime that my mother's religion has always been one of kindness, compassion, and an earnest defense of the weak and troubled. Children, cows, chickens, dogs, cats, and even raccoons have thrived under her loving care.

I took my children to Patrick's Point a year and a half ago. I showed them where Middle Earth was, we all collected agates on the beach, I told them they couldn't bring the seaweed all the way home (which was in Colorado at the time), and I told them about the raccoon. They laughed, and

weren't a bit surprised by Grandma's kindness either. When kindness is the way you live your life, choosing to be kind is easier, wanting to share with even the meanest of animals becomes second nature, and your ability to feel joy increases. I hope when hungry raccoons, love-starved children, and broken-hearted friends come to my door I'll have learned my lessons from her and be able to do what kindness dictates I do. Bind up wounds, speak gentle words, lift a sorrowing heart, and keep an extra loaf of bread or two around for a hungry soul.

Grandma's Steps

Principle #9: Hope is a choice that changes our hearts, slows our steps, and moves us to serve

Grandma Stratton loved shoes. I once delved with her into the depths of her closet and we counted them. There were over 50 pairs...just on one side. I didn't have the energy to dig through the other side since digging entailed taking them out, trying them on, hearing the story of when she got them, where she wore them, etc. We wore the same shoe size which made it doubly fun. I'd put on Grandma's shoes, one of her dresses from the 40s, 50s, or 60s and prance around the house. Grandma never lost her love of playing "dress-up".

Some of her favorite shoes were Keds. She gave me a purple pair and a pink pair when I was fifteen. I loved them. I wore them everywhere. She was known to have red, white, blue, and yellow Keds and probably a rainbow of other colors as well. I found a pair of celery green Ked mules about a year ago in a little second hand shop in Colorado. They were nearly new, and I couldn't pass them up. I slipped those soft, cushy-soled, canvas shoes on and it was like playing dress-up with Grandma all over again. I wore them until the backs were nearly frayed to pieces, but they were still comfortable so I kept right on wearing them. When we moved to Oregon I made sure to pack them in one of the laundry baskets filled with clothes and shoes to make the trip with us but I haven't seen them since we got here. It's been a long time now so I don't suppose they'll show up. It's strange how such a small

thing can break your heart just a little bit. It's one of the reasons we women enjoy shoe shopping. It's not the shoes so much, it's the sorting through options, it's thinking of all the possibilities, it's opening yourself up to all the places you can go and opportunities you can have. And honestly... sometimes it's just about the shoes.

Grandma loved shoes for all those possibilities and more. One of her biggest reasons was the fact that she walked everywhere she went.

There were two causes for this.

One: She loved to walk. She took her time getting places, she admired people's yards, she waved and chatted with people she didn't know, she stopped to enjoy flower gardens. She loved to stroll along the streets in her neighborhood on her way to wherever she was going.

And Two: She never learned to drive. Grandma was incredibly capable. She was smart, funny, personable, adventurous, and kind. I always wondered why she didn't drive; it just seemed so inexplicable to me. Grandpa tried to teach her when they were first married, which apparently hadn't gone very well. My Mom said Grandpa tried to teach her again when she herself was learning in anticipation of getting her license. She didn't elaborate too much beyond laughing and saying, "Poor Mama! She tried to shift the car and nearly took out the garage door. Daddy got frustrated and started yelling, and Mama got mad and started yelling back. She probably could have learned if someone else had taught her."

It's probably true. It makes me chuckle just thinking about it. No one could beat Grandpa for quick-fire frustration, but it never lasted long. And no one could beat Grandma for stubborn obstinacy which could last for years. I can just about hear Grandma's thoughts now; "You won't teach me nicely? FINE. You can drive me wherever I need to go. I don't need to

drive your stupid car to get where I'm going. I'll have a chauffeur."

As far as I know she never tried to learn again, except maybe that once in Yuma, Arizona, when my brothers tried to teach her in a dune buggy. It didn't go very well. Grandma apparently didn't have good luck with garage doors. But her choice to not drive suited them fine. Grandpa enjoyed driving Grandma wherever she was going be it grocery, hairdresser, or mall, and she enjoyed letting him. I think it was one of their small, quiet ways of serving one another and being served which is so essential to a happy marriage.

But when the weather was good, which was often, Grandma would don her shoes and head out for a stroll down Hester Avenue across to Shasta Avenue on toward Brentwood Grocery or down the Alameda to Aki's Bakery. If she was feeling like making it a longer day she'd walk all the way down to the Rosicrucian, past the Rose Garden, and hop a bus out to Vanity Fair. I only went on a shopping trip to the mall with Grandma once or twice, but oh was it fun. I went to the mall in our town just a few times as a teenager. I wasn't a regular mall junkie, looking for a place to hang out for awhile. There was usually something specific I needed and I would run in and run out. It was only during the holidays that I spent any real time there. But shopping with Grandma was a whole different experience.

She worked in women's retail nearly her whole adult life so she knew a lot about clothes, shoes, jewelry, purses, and all things feminine. She knew what was quality and what was junk, and she wasn't afraid to try things on that she had absolutely no intention of buying.

That was half the fun of shopping for her. It wasn't the purchasing and possessing so much as the possibilities the items themselves represented. We walked for hours around Vanity Fair, trying on shoes, costume jewelry, skirts, scarves, and dresses. We pranced around with purses big enough to fit a Great Dane in and little jeweled clutches that made me think

of Grace Kelly or Audrey Hepburn. We sat in little café chairs and sipped pink lemonade while we people watched.

"People are so fascinating," Grandma would say. "It's so fun just to sit and watch them."

When it was time to head home, we'd hop another bus and wind our way back through the city until we walked again past the lovely blossoms and fragrance of the Rose Garden and up the wide brick steps of the Jungle House.

Grandma learned to love walking early on, and I think her adventurous spirit was as much hereditary as it was innate. Her Grandma Stowe had set out in a farm wagon from Faribault, Minnesota, with just her 4-year-old son Arthur to join her husband in California in the late 1800s. He had gone west to seek work and a chance to improve their situation. She decided after he left that she was more concerned with being together than she was with their financial position so against everyone's advice but what she felt in her own heart, she packed up her wagon and her child, hitched up her team of horses, and crossed the prairies, mountains, and deserts of western America all on her own.

Oh how I wish I had more of her story. I can only imagine what it was like to make that trip, what kind of bravery it took and determination. She was a woman I would love to know better. Her son Arthur never lost the love of travel that the trip across the continent had given him. As a grown and married man he found work as a foreman in the orchards, vineyards, and fields of farmers all up and down the great central valley of California. He spoke English, Spanish, some Portuguese and a spattering of other languages. It was enough to help him negotiate wages and work between laborers and land owners. My Grandma, little red-haired Vivian, had two lively feet and she would by turns walk, dance, or run beside their wagon up and down the farm roads of California during the beginning days of its booming agricultural industry.

90

Apparently Grandpa Stowe learned to drive also, but never caught on. My Grandma's brother, Cecil, bought a Model T Ford and took Grandpa Stowe out to the cliffs near Monterey to teach him to drive. What possessed him to try and teach Grandpa on some cliffs is beyond my powers of comprehension. I think they took a trip out to see the ocean and it was more a case of "here we are, let's teach you to drive" than anything else.

Grandpa did fine shifting the car into the different gears and working the gas pedal, steering it too, but when it came to the brake he couldn't quite manage it. As they neared the cliff, Cecil said, "You'd better slow down now, Pop." To which Arthur said "Whoa," and then louder "Whoa!" He didn't quite understand that the Model T wasn't designed to pick up on voice commands and all the while Cecil was yelling "Put on the brake! Put on the brake!", Grandpa was yelling, "Whoa, damn it! I said whoa!"

Cecil finally shoved Grandpa back and put on the brake himself. The car sputtered and died, and Grandpa climbed out swearing he would never drive one of those contraptions again while Cecil roared with laughter. Grandpa figured horses were cheaper anyway. When they ran out of "gas" you just pulled to the side of the road and let them fill up again on grass; it didn't cost a dime.

One of the groups of laborers my Grandpa Arthur worked with were the Gypsies. He spoke a little Romany and could find them work and make sure they were paid. I don't know whether it was cultural prejudice or from personal experience, but he had a terrible distrust of the Gypsy people. And though they worked together in the fields, they didn't socialize around the campfire. But Vivian was fascinated by them. She would tell us as children about how late at night, after they had tethered their horses to graze, put out their own fire, and climbed in bed, she would stay awake listening to the gypsy music and watch their fires and figures dance and flicker through the dark trees. She loved the sound and the movement. It began a life-long love affair with music and

91

dancing. She dreamed of being a Broadway star while she ironed laundry for a nickel a load as a teenager. She would hoard her pennies all week and spend them on a Saturday matinee and popcorn at the theater where she watched the Radio City Music Hall Rockettes dance their way across the screen. Then she'd run home and practice pouting like Clara Bow in her bathroom mirror and wear lipstick that was too red and eye shadow that was too blue.

She told me once that she drove her mother crazy all the time. She waved her hands in the air and said "I was star crazed! I was going to run off to Broadway and be a famous dancer. My poor mother! She'd say "Vivian! Quit dancing all over the house!"

I love picturing her like that; young, red hair in ringlets, dancing the Charleston on her way down the street to pick up laundry. I think we would have been grand friends had we been young together. As it is we were grand friends though there were nearly 60 years between us. But what are a few years between friends anyway?

By the time I was old enough to dance down streets with her she was doing what we called the "Granny Shuffle." She loved to walk but she didn't stride like someone in a hurry. She walked with small, short steps, her hands always busy holding mine or waving at someone on the street. It appeared to me that she knew everyone and she was friendly with all, even with people she didn't particularly like. She told my mother when she was young, "Janice, a third of the people you meet in this life you'll get along with, another third you won't, and the last third you'll feel ambivalent about. You may not like all the people you meet, but you can be nice no matter what. There's no reason to be unkind just because you disagree or don't get along."

I love those little gems of wisdom.

I walked so many places with my Grandma. One of my favorites was Shasta Avenue, just one street over from Hester Avenue where Grandma lived. Oh how I loved that street. I'm not a city girl at heart, but I was charmed by the homes there. One home in particular was our favorite. Grandma called it "Snow White's Cottage." It had a high, steep, tile-covered roof, ivy on the stucco walls, and a rounded top door. I wanted to live there. I wanted to live with the ivy and the flowers blooming in the front yard and be the one who walked through that rounded door every morning to pick roses from the front step and bring them inside to arrange in pretty vases by the small-paned windows in the kitchen where I would make tea cakes to serve with pink lemonade. Then Grandma and I would sit under the big oak in the front yard, sip lemonade, nibble cakes, and show each other our new shoes. It was a marvelous little dream, and to this day whenever I see a house that resembles our little cottage, or a rounded door, I feel a pang of homesickness for it. I've always felt you couldn't help but have a happy ending in a place that belonged in a fairytale.

> A third of the people you meet in this life you'll get along with, another third you won't, and the last third you'll feel ambivalent about. You may not like all the people you meet, but you can be nice no matter what. There's no reason to be unkind just because you disagree or don't get along.

I'm amazed now as an adult at the path my Grandma walked and more than ever I am grateful for the steps she took.

It couldn't have been easy as a thirty year old to find herself wondering if her husband would survive the terrible accident he had, and if he did, how would she care for him? And if he didn't, how would she care for her children? She could have given in to fear, to despair, to grief. I'm certain she had many tear filled, prayerful nights throughout that first year and the many that followed. But she didn't give in; she chose hope.

She believed, and I believe also, that hope is a choice we make no matter how dire the circumstances. That hope doesn't change the future but rather it changes our hearts. And a change of heart leads to a change in our actions and action CAN change our future. How we think and the will we exert to change our thinking from negative to positive changes things for us.

My life has become terribly busy compared to the days of strolling down Shasta Avenue in San Jose or walking up the driveway at Hillcrest Orchards to look at the real Mt. Shasta and the valley below it with Grandma. I'm so busy driving, delivering, picking up, and dropping off that I don't take time to walk past rose gardens much. It's a shame, or worse it's very nearly a sin considering how much I love to take my time looking at things. It's one of the greatest blessings of farm life that there are some things that simply can't be rushed. A chicken will lay an egg as fast or as slow as it wants; it refuses to be hurried along. A cow cannot be milked too fast, or it will hurt her udder so we take our time. A new calf will be born when it's good and ready and not a moment before. Crops grow slowly, their speed determined by the sun, the warmth of the soil, the rain, and the passage of time.

I am compelled by my profession to slow down, to take my time, observe, record, and refine my thinking so that the next crop or calf is healthier.

How much more admirable my grandmother was that she chose to slow her steps when it would have appeared more prudent to speed them up in order to accomplish the work of both father and mother. How infinitely more precious was her decision to choose hope, in a world that would have condoned her despair, in the face of her trials. How glorious and miraculous was her ability to find joy in simple things: rose petals, leaves blowing across a tidy city street, dandelions in a child's hand, orange peels from a child who had eaten all of the orange and had nothing else to give but a sincere desire to share, a call from a friend, beautiful things displayed in a

shop window, a warm drink on a cool morning, and a cold drink on a warm afternoon.

Joy filled Grandma's life not because she was luckier than most, more beautiful, wealthier, or smarter, but because she chose to see it. It's there all around us all the time; we just have to open our eyes to see it, our ears to hear it, and our hearts to feel it. It's a difficult choice because when you open your heart to joy so many other feelings rush in as well.

Awareness, the quality of having an alert mind, allows us to experience an increase in joy and sorrow, in beauty and horror, in rapture and grief. In order to know one, you must accept the other. It's a necessary step to living fully, to getting as close to a "perfect" life as we ever can. There's no way to understand what perfect joy is without understanding perfect pain. Pain is the process by which perfection is born. It cannot be contrived; it cannot be replaced by an adrenaline rush or gained from sitting in a theater. To be understood it has to involve your whole heart. I think Grandma Stratton understood perfect pain. She experienced it time and again in her life: when she watched her childhood friend Little Ethel being laid to rest in a tiny grave; when she struggled through the agony of childbirth to bring her son and her daughter into the world; when she stood by the bedside of her torn, shattered, and broken husband. Yes, she understood pain. It is a universal gift that every human being experiences. We cannot live without it and we cannot avoid it.

But hope...hope is our choice. Hope is an exercise of our free will that stretches our spirit when we think it will break, enlarges our heart when we think it can bear no more, and opens our mind to see around the pain that is within us. From that seed of hope joy grows, a tiny burgeoning belief that there is something better. Better days, deeper feelings, and broader horizons. And as it grows, the brightness of that joy illuminates our path and suddenly we find that beauty was with us all along, love never left us even when we felt alone, forgotten and abandoned, and that we are stronger than we knew we could be.

That is the path Grandma walked with her short steps and happy hands. That is the power of her choice and her legacy. I remember her life and I think: if Grandma could walk a little out of her way in order to find beauty and spread joy, what am I doing today to make that kind of difference?

I am grateful that Grandma and I share the same size feet, it makes me try harder to walk in her footsteps and fill her shoes.

Goose Pen

Principle #10: We all make mistakes and we all need help to overcome them

Geese are mean. I'll get that out of my system right here and now. They are lovely. They are wonderful guards for chickens. They can even shepherd a flock of sheep. But they are also mean. They chase, they bite (well, they don't actually have teeth, just a bill, so it's more of a pinch than a bite), and they can beat you up with their wings. I can say this with certainty and conviction because I learned all about geese first-hand when I was six years old.

We had a very diverse farm at Hillcrest Orchards. We had dairy and beef cattle. We had chickens, turkeys, pigs, horses, a peacock, an ever-changing array of farm dogs, an old barn cat (who was named very un-originally "Tom," which I suppose ranks right up there with "Blue" in the clever name department), and a few geese. I don't know where the geese came from or why we had them. We lived in a farming community where animals and farm goods were traded back and forth on a regular basis so it's possible we acquired them in a swap somewhere along the line.

They had a pen beside the low-sloped eaves of the old, red, western-style barn but more often than not they had free roam of the farm. They ranged far and wide, eating bugs, toads, snails, weeds, anything that was newly sprouted in the garden, and berries off the wild and thorny blackberry bushes. I didn't pay much attention to them as they waddled their way

97

around the farm. They always moved in a pack, were awfully noisy, and that was the extent of my interest in them. But then one day when we were walking past the barn to the building that housed the cider press, the authority figure with me (it could have been any one of a number of people: Mom, Dad, Debbie, Kris, Roger, Kirk, Joy) said just as we passed it, "Don't go in the goose pen."

I must be contrary by nature. It never occurred to me to ever go in the goose pen before they said it. I didn't really care about the geese; they were just a little blip on my personal interest radar. But suddenly now that the "don't go in the goose pen" gauntlet had been thrown down, they were suddenly my target. I was caught up in a burning desire to go in the goose pen. I had to know. "Why?" I wondered. "Why shouldn't I go in the goose pen?" After all, I had crossed the pasture where Knuckles the Jersey bull was kept without getting killed (which is a miracle in itself), why couldn't I handle a couple of silly geese?

It ate at me. The desire to go in the goose pen took over my little brain. The battle to obey and the curiosity of a child became an epic battle of good over evil in my head and finally I made my decision.

I was going in.

I didn't know when the opportunity to commit this heinous crime would present itself, but I waited until it did. Six-year-old girls are seldom left all alone on a farm, Mom is usually watching from a window, Dad is right around the corner, or several brothers are there being obnoxious while you are busy contemplating being devious. But patience paid off, and the opportunity presented itself one morning bright and dearly before the sun had even risen.

Chores started early, but not usually for me. Dad, Ken, Kirk, and Kris were always up before the sun—Dad willingly, the others not quite as willing. They milked our Guernsey cows by hand, gathered eggs, and tended to the other animals

while Mom made breakfast and got Aaron, Jared, and me ready to catch the bus to school. It always seemed that after breakfast there was time to play before the school bus arrived, for a few minutes anyway, so I took advantage of it.

It was cold outside. I don't remember the day or month, but I recall that it was gray and cold. I'm sure it's one of God's tender mercies that I attempted this planned disobedience on a day when I was bundled up in my blue Holly Hobbie coat and my knit cap. They came in handy as a defense.

We were all in the farmyard doing various things that I'm sure were important at the time when I looked around to see if anyone was nearby. Ah ha! Luck was with me, even if prudence was not, and I couldn't see anybody. I started to climb the wooden slats of the goose pen while they looked on in benign silence. I think I had some vision of becoming the Goose Girl from the old fairy tale, the one where the horse gets its head chopped off but still talks to the goose girl who is really a princess in disguise. It's a terribly gruesome story when you come to think of it; a sick marriage of Snow White and the Godfather. That should have been a warning right there, but I was well beyond warnings. I swung my leg over the top rail, swung the other leg over as well, took one last look around and dropped into the goose pen.

This was no fairy tale my friends. Those silent, benign geese of only moments before became screeching, flapping fiends sent from the bowels of Hades to torment the sinner. They plucked at my coat, hitting me hard enough to knock me back into the fence railing; they beat at me with their wings and pecked at my knit cap and my hair. Again and again they pecked at me and knocked me down while I tried to muster up enough breath to scream.

I finally hollered at the top of my lungs and hit out at them with my own hands which didn't do anything but make them peck at my sleeves and screech louder themselves. They had me backed into a corner of the pen by the barn and the

fence rail. I remember sobbing and screaming and thinking how much I hated geese when I looked over and saw my brother Kris come running across the farmyard towards me. I don't think Andromeda facing the Kraken or Guinevere tied to the stake seeing Lancelot on his charger were more relieved than I was at that moment to see my teenage brother come sailing across the fence in his Wranglers and canvas work coat. He kicked at the geese that screeched at him but ran to the far side of the pen, picked me up by the back of my coat and with sincere brotherly affection said:

"What's wrong with you? Are you stupid? What did you go in the goose pen for?"

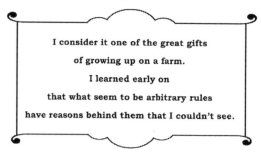

I consider it one of the great gifts of growing up on a farm. I learned early on that what seem to be arbitrary rules have reasons behind them that I couldn't see.

He tossed me out of the pen, half disgusted that I needed rescuing in the first place and half grateful that I wasn't hurt, just scared.

As for myself, I was so grateful to have been saved from the clutches of Hades' goose herd that I could only agree with him. Yes, yes I was stupid and I have no earthly reason to give you for why I went into the pen.

It was a painful lesson, but I'm grateful I had it at six. I'm grateful it was only geese I decided to be disobedient about, and more than anything I'm grateful that my brother was there to save me, to chastise me, and to set me back on solid ground.

I've had other moments of disobedience in my life, but never that premeditated. I consider it one of the great gifts of growing up on a farm. I learned early on that what seem to be arbitrary rules have reasons behind them that I couldn't see. I learned to trust that my parents didn't say "no" because they wanted to make me miserable, they didn't say "stay away" just to keep me from having fun. They really did love me, they

really did want me to be happy, and they really could see more of the dangers that I faced than I could. By virtue of having lived longer, by experiencing more, and having a few run-ins with geese themselves, they know what would happen to me in the Goose Pen. I learned to trust them.

And I gained a much needed dose of humility. Sometimes you get yourself into a situation that you simply don't know how to get out of by yourself. It would be easy to say with worldly logic "She got herself into that mess, she can get herself out." Thank God my brother possessed more mercy than that worldly reasoning. I couldn't get myself out. Yes, it was a situation of my own making; yes, I probably deserved to get pecked by the geese. But isn't it wonderful that while my brother knew I had been stupid to go into the pen, he was also able to have enough compassion to pull me out? Just because people make mistakes and they have "earned" the fate that befalls them does not relieve us of the responsibility of compassion.

All of us have faced our own goose pens. All of us have allowed, at one time or another, curiosity to get the better of our common sense and given in to stupidity. It's a slippery slope downhill from curiosity to stupidity, from stupidity to fear, and from fear to pain. And it's so hard when you are afraid and in pain to step back and be reasonable, to be able to make better choices.

All I had to do was climb out of the goose pen and I would have been fine. But I was so overcome by fear of the geese and their pinching beaks that I couldn't even tell that I was standing right next to my way out. It took the leap of faith my brother made over the fence to pull me out again. I'm still grateful. Thanks Kris.

Oh, and I still hate geese.

Jungle House

Principle #11: Small daily choices are the things upon which our lives are built: choose well

My Grandpa, Wilton Allen Stratton, was born in Big Bend, Wisconsin, the oldest son of a Stratton and a Frazer, both descendants of Scottish Covenanters who fled the much-loved shores of their homeland in search of the freedom and the chance to own out-right the land they farmed. The blood of highland rebels and early American patriots ran strong and true in his veins. His father William fell in love with photography early on in his life and as a family we are lucky enough to have an assortment of photos and unusual photographic keepsakes. My favorite is a photo of my 3-year-old, curly-headed grandpa asleep on the back step of their home. His chubby hand is curled up by his face, his bottom is wet (as a young child's bottom often is), and his little leather boots are unlaced. He is such a picture of freckle-faced youth, worn out from play that I have made an enlarged copy of it and it hangs in my home today.

I love my Grandpa. I don't say "loved" even though he has been gone now for over 20 years because the brilliance and power of the love I feel for him has not diminished in all that time. If anything it simply burns brighter. I warn all readers right here that this particular love letter will be unapologetically sentimental, affectionate, and emotional. I hope all of you can read about my grandfather and be reminded of the love of your own grandfather. If you can't,

then simply take a lesson from him and choose to BE the kind of grandparent he was.

Growing up all of his friends called him "Red" for obvious reasons: he had red hair. Curly, red hair and freckles. I might be inclined to say "poor kid" but he was anything but. If curly, red-hair ever suited anyone, it was Grandpa. I didn't know him as a child but I've heard his stories, seen his photo books, and knew enough of him as an old man that I can guess what he was like as a youth: rambunctious, a little wild, a hard worker, brave. He was the kind of youth that wanted to climb peaks, conquer the sea, and build a home with his own two hands.

As soon as he was able to walk he was helping in the family's farm fields. His father raised chickens, ducks, eggs, melons, and squash for markets in Milwaukee, Wisconsin. William Aaron Stratton was a good farmer. Every year he saved seeds from the melons that had the smallest cavities and the sweetest flavor. He saved seed from the biggest watermelons with the sweetest taste and the most sugary texture. He developed such good varieties that buyers in the city started asking for his melons by name. One year he even grew all the melons for the Wisconsin State Fair. He was proud of his labors. This was no dirt-poor farmer or peasant plow-boy; his forefathers had given up their homeland so that he could be a free landowner and he never took it for granted. It took him years of laboring in rented fields to finally be able to buy 20 acres and a home on the spring-fed pond in the countryside out of the town of Big Bend. It was the same land where I stood half a century later with my great-aunt Sybil, Grandpa's oldest sister.

20 acres doesn't sound like much now when modern farmers are planting and harvesting such vast fields that it's sometimes impossible to see from one side to the other. But it was all he needed to provide a good living for his family. He was pleased to raise his family in the heart of his new homeland. He dreamed of passing a legacy of freedom onto his children and a love of heritage. His parents slept in the

Covenanter cemetery just down the road and someday he would do the same. He had found his place in the world, he shared it with the woman he loved, and he taught his children to love it also. And love it they did. Though they toiled under brutally hot summer sunshine and through bitterly cold Wisconsin winters, they didn't despise the toil. It was simply their place and their way.

Yes my Grandpa Red loved the farm. He loved racing the neighboring farm boys up and down the frozen pond on ice skates, daring each other to get just a little closer to the thin spots near where the spring bubbled up. He loved playing baseball on muggy summer evenings when the days work was done and before night chores. As he got older he loved the challenge of organized sports. I have pictures of him decked out in basketball and football uniforms and a favorite one of him standing next to an old motorcycle with a sidecar. Written in white ink on the old faded black and white print are the words "Wilton's First Harley." I can just picture him racing up and down the back country roads, setting up a cloud of dust and old tongues wagging on his way to see friends; the ache to see, to do, to "become" growing inside him every year as sure and as steady as the seasons that chased each other around the months.

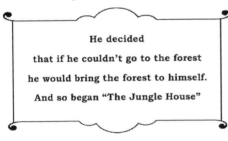

He decided that if he couldn't go to the forest he would bring the forest to himself. And so began "The Jungle House"

Grandpa had the soul of an adventurer; he grew up on tales of the West—of wild mountain men and wilder Indians, great mountain ranges, grand canyons, and trees as tall as the sky. He wanted to see it all. He wanted to stand in the surf of the Pacific Ocean, he wanted to hike forests that had been saplings when Julius Caesar was conquering the world, and he wanted to see the endless expanse that was America in the mid 1920s.

Though his parents were rooted in their place, they understood their son's need to go out and find his own. I think they hoped he would find it there near them, but that was not to be. It was their oldest daughter Sybil who thrived in that deep, glacial till soil.

The sweet, freckle-faced boy became an independent, auburn-haired young man in search of himself. He hopped a train in Milwaukee with a good friend and together they rode the railroad all across the West. Through the Black Hills of south Dakota, across Yellowstone, and the Teton Mountain range he rode along propelled ever westward by the mighty steam engine through cities bursting into new life and across parched and barren deserts where it seemed impossible that anything could survive to the emerald cathedral forests of western Washington state and at long last the rough and wild coastline of the northwestern Pacific shore.

He loved it all.

All the grandeur, barrenness, beauty, and simplicity were intricate portions of what this country meant to him. He went in search of it and more than just searching for it he opened his heart to it. So that when the majesty that was America struck him it had fertile soil to grow in his soul.

He had an uncle and cousins in Washington with whom he visited and more in Santa Clara, California. It was expected that if he made it all the way to the Evergreen State he was certainly able to visit the Golden one as well; and so he did, drinking in the views of Oregon along the way.

Here is the part of the story where everything changed for young Wilton. There in the upper Central Valley of California Grandpa fell in love: twice.

The first time was with the fertile fields, pastures, orchards, and vineyards of the San Joaquin Valley. He couldn't believe that any place on the planet could be that rich in the good things of the Earth. The second time was with a young, fiery-haired (and tempered) girl of Irish extraction named

Vivian Stowe. She was no shy lass and they struck sparks off each other from the day they met until the end of their lives, he in 1987 and Grandma in 1998.

She often told stories of how they liked to tease him when he first arrived in California. There were fruits and vegetables growing there that he had never seen or heard of before and they would talk him into trying all of them...when they weren't ripe yet. I think it's a testament to his resiliency that he overcame his first impressions and went on to eat and eventually grow some of those fruits right in his own backyard.

He stayed in California for a little while but eventually headed back north to Washington where his Uncle Vernon lived and who had agreed to help him attend Forestry School.

It was the thing that he wanted to do more than anything, to spend his time in and amongst the trees. The lumber industry was growing along with the national desire to preserve some of the pristine wilderness that has left countless pioneers and visitors awestruck. Grandpa himself was very conservation minded and wanted to help find a balance between the growing needs of society and the preservation of the beauty of the wild. He considered it a matter of good stewardship and his heart belonged to the trees.

While I was growing up, he would often tell my brothers and me about his mother, about how petite she was but how hard she worked. He told us about what a good mother she was to him and how much he missed her. Even then, as an old man in his 70's he would get tears in his eyes for the memory of his mother.

It's impossible to know when you're in your early 20s the impact that one decision can have on your life. Grandpa's decision to leave Wisconsin changed his life, enlarged his mind, his desires, and his opportunities; his decision to return changed his life again.

Uncle Vernon had agreed to pay for his schooling. He had been accepted to the university and everything was in order for him to begin his schooling in the spring semester when the unexpected and heartbreaking happened. A call came from Wisconsin. Nettie Alice Frazer Stratton had risen that morning to go out and milk her cows then sat back down on the bed saying "I don't feel well." She lay back on her pillows and never stirred again. Her heart, long troubled and laboring from congenital heart disease had finally given out.

It was a heartbreak which always plagued Grandpa, that he never had a chance to see her again before she died. He often felt guilty that he had left to pursue his own interests and hadn't been there to help shoulder the burdens of the farm. But she wouldn't have wanted that. As a mother myself I can speak with conviction and certainty that she would have wanted her son to find his own place in the world, to find his own home and build his own dream. She had lived her dream and lived it fully. Can there be a greater gift to a woman who cherished the land she labored on than to be able to work in harmony with it until the day she died and then to be enveloped in its embrace?

There was no question in Wilton's mind whether he would return to Big Bend for the funeral; of course he would go, he must go. But Uncle Vernon disagreed. Grandpa never discussed the disagreement in detail but nearly half a century later the decision Vernon made could still upset him: stay and I'll pay for school. Go home and you're on your own.

I can't pretend to understand Vernon. I never knew him after all. Perhaps he thought Wilton would never come back to finish his schooling if he went home. Perhaps he saw no need to stand by the grave of a lifeless corpse, no matter how cherished the life had been. No, I don't understand his reasons, but I knew my grandfather well enough to know that there could be only one decision. Home he went with a weight on his heart from the knowledge that when he arrived the person who had given "home" all its meaning would not be there to welcome him.

The fields were covered with snow when he stepped off the train and the little Covenanter cemetery was blanketed peacefully with its weight. Lovingly, the hands that a small, simple, but great woman had guided to adulthood tended to that which she could not do for herself and prepared for her the last bed in which she would rest. There are pictures of Grandpa's family at the funeral. There is sadness in my Grandpa's eyes that hadn't been there before and an acceptance in Great-Grandpa William's eyes that shows the knowledge of a man who understood on an intimate level the cycle of life and death, sowing and reaping, and recognized his place in it. Grandpa's sorrow was tremendous but the lessons he had learned early at his mother's side in the farm fields stood him in good stead; after every harvest and time of rest there comes the season of planting again.

So Wilton began again, this time in an old Model "something or other" Ford (a car aficionado would be able to tell me what kind of car is in the pictures) he set off again. This time directly to California and where he knew his future lay. He stopped and worked at farms along the way to buy the gas he needed to run the car, finally pulling into San Jose after several weeks of driving.

His opportunity to attend forestry school with the help of family was gone, but his determination to go had not ebbed. He found work and began saving. Along the way he married his fiery-haired Vivian, the girl with the gypsy feet, and together they welcomed Frazer and Janice into the world. Wilton read, studied, worked, and searched for opportunities to further his knowledge, but his desire to attend school kept getting pushed further and further down on his list of priorities. World War II changed the routine and tenor of daily life for their family. The brickyard where Grandpa ran a steam shovel stepped up production to help feed the war effort. His early experiences on the farm helped when rationing became a hardship for them. They raised a garden full of produce and raised rabbits for meat on a little quarter-acre lot on Hester Avenue and traded with a network of other like-minded friends and family for butter, eggs, and milk.

I have another picture of Grandpa that I love. In this one, taken around 1941, he is standing strong and firm, his forearms well-muscled and his shoulders broad, evidence of the physical labors he performed. My uncle Frado is standing in front of him, a cute, curly-haired boy of three or four, and my Grandma is standing beside him holding a tiny, bundled-up baby which grew up to be my mom. I love this picture; it is how I picture my Grandpa even though it is not how I knew him. I look at that picture and I see traces of my brothers and myself in his face and my Grandma's. I see a good man quietly dedicated to doing what had to be done to care for his family.

It's amazing really how dedication to completing small tasks well can have the greatest impact on our lives. A father who daily performs the work that provides his family with sustenance, a mother who patiently tends to all of the seemingly inconsequential catastrophes her children face, teaching them to stick with it and be patient, that life isn't a race, it's a steady climb towards our goals.

Those were the lessons Wilton and Vivian were teaching their children in 1944 when inattention to a small detail altered their lives forever.

Grandpa ran the steam shovel in the brickyard but he also helped haul bricks from where they were formed to the kilns where they were fired. He would stack 50 lbs of bricks into a hod and carry them across a narrow catwalk type bridge that spanned part of the quarry where they dug out the clay for the bricks. There were man holes at various places along the bridge where ladders were positioned for workers to climb up to the kilns. In a tragic series of small choices, another employee climbed one of the ladders removed the manhole covering so that he could get through, and forgot to cover it again just minutes before my grandfather set out across the bridge. He had a full load of bricks in his arms, making it impossible for him to see the walkway in front of him.

I hate thinking of what happened next. It's physically painful. With no way of knowing he was not safe Grandpa

kept walking and stepped right into the empty space. It was large enough that he fell, bricks and all, almost 50 feet to the bottom of the quarry floor.

He was shattered. Literally shattered.

The doctors told my Grandma that the bones in his legs and feet had been shattered so completely that there was no way he could walk again, if he even lived, which they doubted he would. My mother remembers not knowing what had happened but that it was something terrible. The pastor of their church came to visit, her grandma and grandpa Stowe came to the house to stay with her and Frado. Aunts, uncles, cousins and friends came and gathered together with the family awaiting news.

Miraculously he survived the fall and the first few days in the hospital, but his prognosis was terrible. The doctors were convinced that he would be bedridden or wheel-chair bound for the rest of his life. But they didn't know my Grandpa.

For over a year he laid in a hospital bed in San Francisco, unable to see his children because no children were allowed, only seeing Vivian once a week because she had to find work to make ends meet. It would have been the perfect time to sink into despair and self-pity, to wallow in how unfair his lot was, and to cast blame wherever he could. He had friends who encouraged him to do just that.

"Why don't you sue the brickyard?" they asked. "It's their fault you're crippled now. You ought to at least get something out of it."

"What would I get out of it?" he would ask in return. "It won't give me back my legs. All it would do is put my friends out of business. It wasn't their fault; it was just a mistake that led to a terrible accident." He believed beyond any doubt that his life had been spared for a reason, and he refused to believe that his value as a person was tied to the strength of a couple of bones.

111

When he was released from the hospital and came home he was still bedridden. He had some friends come over and build a pulley system he had designed over his bed. With it he exercised every day. His strength had diminished but he was determined to prove the doctors wrong and his own heart right. Every day he worked his upper and lower body, he built braces that attached to his shoes which would support him since his legs could not. He carved canes for himself that fit his grip perfectly. They became an extension of himself and he wielded them well. The body he had known all his adult life was gone but he never took for granted what remained.

But a body as weakened as his was couldn't be worked all day long and there were countless hours that needed to be filled. Grandpa chose to fill them with books. I have never met anyone as well read as my grandfather. One of the first topics he pursued was his original educational goal: forestry. He studied the works and lives of the great naturalists of the world. He came to know intimately the wide variety of trees and plants that filled the western mountains.

Weeks and months passed. His health improved to the point that he could stand with crutches and canes. A picture of their family during this time shows my grandfather much as I remembered him, his face worn by physical pain, a body weakened by injury, but still that determined look in the eyes. His body shattered that day at the bottom of the quarry, but not his spirit.

He went back to work in the brickyard with braces rigged up to hold his feet to the pedals of the steam shovel. Grandma kept working at Hart's department store and together they kept going as a family. They both had too much tenacity, high hopes, and what Grandpa called "Yankee Pluck" to ever give up on themselves, on life, and on living it fully.

Grandpa knew he would never be able to hike the mountains as he had done so often before but he still longed for them. He especially longed for the trees. He loved the

wild abandon of the forest flora, the dense green of the deep glades and the beautiful patterns cast by leaf-dappled sunlight. He decided that if he couldn't go to the forest he would bring the forest to himself. And so began "The Jungle House."

I think it started with palm trees in the front yard, but not tall palms. These were the low-growing, large frond, fat trunk variety. They grew and they grew, and then they grew some more. Grandpa kept the walkway in front of the house cleared but as the various vines, palms, pines, and other plants he brought home flourished it soon became more of a tunnel than a walkway. By the time I came along some thirty years later the house truly was in the midst of a jungle. We could always tell which house was Grandma's because there wasn't a house there; just trees and vines. Wild plums and loquats thrived in the backyard. We picked and ate them whenever we visited.

Grandpa planted a pine tree in his backyard the year I was born. We took turns being the tallest for a number of years until we hit five years old and it surpassed me for good. It grew to over 30 feet tall before the new home owners decided to cut it down after Grandma moved to my Mom and Dad's house in 1997.

Deciding moments come to us almost every day. Small decisions can lead to enormous consequences and the fear of what will be can become almost staggering to a person plagued by indecision. But decide we must; for to live in indecision is to turn your back on life. The power to choose for ourselves is at the heart of what makes us human. Sometimes we choose poorly, sometimes well. Sometimes we choose something good because we are afraid there will be no "better" to come along. Sometimes we feel we have no choice in our decisions simply because one or more of our choices is so untenable to us.

As an adult I can look back at my Grandpa's choices and be, quite simply, staggered by them. I am awed by his

113

selfless spirit. In a day and age when self-fulfillment and self-satisfaction are rewarded, applauded, and encouraged, his life would be something of an anachronism. He didn't seek his own ease, nor did my Grandmother. I wish I could express the dedication it took for him to just keep living, let alone all the other good he did in his life with his limited mobility.

Just to keep living required tremendous effort. Every step he took from the day of his accident to the day of his death over 40 years later was taken through pain. It hurt him to stand, it hurt him to walk, but he kept standing and he kept walking. The braces on his shoes would rub his legs raw and no socks were thick enough to protect them; so he learned to knit. I love that about him. He didn't complain because someone else didn't know how to make a sock thick enough to protect his legs or his nerve-damaged feet. He picked up a how-to book and a couple of knitting needles and he did it himself.

Because of the damage done to not only his legs but the rest of his body as well he suffered from problems with digestion, kidney pain, and just simply breathing. He didn't wait for someone else to come up with a cure for him. He read, studied, and pondered the human body. He started taking vitamin and mineral supplements long before it was en vogue to do so. A doctor once told him to keep up whatever he was doing because his heart was as healthy as a horse's.

Throughout his life Wilton A. Stratton suffered heartbreaking losses and disappointments, but he never quit. If his heart was broken, it didn't diminish from the pain, it simply made room for greater empathy and more love for others. If he lost the full use of his legs, it was only to be replaced by a before unknown strength in his arms. Knowing him the way I do I believe that if he hadn't had the use of his arms, he would have hung onto life with his teeth.

He traversed the western fields he had come to love as a young man later on in his life from a car. Several summers were spent driving his teenaged children back and

forth to Wisconsin and up and down the California coasts and mountains. He watched the deep fertile fields of the San Joaquin Valley disappear beneath layers of asphalt and concrete. It made him sad. He loved to drive; he had more mobility then, and he went everywhere he could in a car. He would drive along what had once been small country lanes and pull over to the side of the road. Where now there stood shiny new subdivision homes he would point and say "this used to be a grove of cherry trees" or sometimes apricot and plum. "It's a shame they cut it down. Someday they'll be sorry that they covered up the most fertile ground in the world."

As he got older his ability to go and do diminished, but never his drive to give. He was forever sending us books, newspaper clippings or magazine articles that he found interesting. My husband's brother does the same and he has a special place in my heart because of it.

We were living in Yuma, Arizona when Grandpa got sick for the last time with prostate cancer. My Mom woke up one morning and said "I need to go home to Mom and Daddy. I don't know what's wrong, but I need to go home." She flew to San Jose the next day and she was there for two weeks. Grandpa died at home while she was there, right where he wanted to be, surrounded by those he loved and who loved him.

My Grandpa Johnson died when I was eight years old, I knew that Birgit, my Dad's first wife, and their daughter Cynthia had died before I was even born, but this was the first time death had reached me on a truly personal level. I hadn't known Grandpa Johnson well enough to mourn very much, and I hadn't known Birgit and Cynthia at all, but I knew Grandpa Stratton. I couldn't imagine the world without him in it.

I couldn't look at him right away, lying in a casket, so I wandered the halls of the funeral home. It was so hushed and quiet there, as if people were afraid to talk too loud. I wanted

to yell "Talk as loud as you want! They're not going to wake up!" But I didn't. I stepped into another room; chapels are what they called them, which I suppose is why we were reverent. Inside this one there was a tiny casket. The room was empty but for that small, white, lace-covered coffin. My breath got stuck in my lungs as I stood there and I finally had to sob to get them breathing again. It struck me how wrong the size of that casket was; how absolutely wrong it was for a newborn to die when there was so much of life to be lived.

But, wrong or not, it is life. Grandpa knew it and, though it was a bitter understanding to accept, I knew it too. Some harvests come sooner than others, some seasons are so short that they seem to hardly exist at all. But they are there and though they are short they are beautiful.

I thought of those two souls traveling together, away for a time from family, and I was suddenly grateful that the tiny soul, whose earthly form rested there on that podium, had someone as strong, as true, and as brave as my grandfather to walk with her. I believe things like that. In a world where nothing is real that can't be proven in a Petri dish or measured on a scale I know it sounds odd, but some of the most real things in life are those which can't be measured or seen under a microscope.

We buried Grandpa on a cool spring morning at Oak Hill Cemetery in San Jose. My Mom found a beautiful casket made of carved wood. It seemed appropriate for a man who had been most at home in the forests, amidst the trees. I don't remember anything after the funeral. I suppose I was too consumed with my own grief to think of much else. But I do remember the next time we visited Grandma's house. I didn't know what I'd feel, what to expect when one of the people who made it "home" was gone. But

> Some harvests come sooner than others, some seasons are so short that they seem to hardly exist at all. But they are there and though they are short they are beautiful.

it was still the same. Grandma was still there with her sweet smell and fiery-red hair now gone white. And Grandpa was there too. As we walked through the Jungle House canopy of trees I could feel his touch on everything. In the backyard the squirrels were still living in the trees he had planted. Grandma was faithfully leaving walnuts out for them every morning. He was still there in the garage where his woodworking tools were hung up collecting dust.

Grandma changed things over the years after Grandpa passed away. She gave the tools to a young woodworker whom she knew; she had the wild disarray of the jungle tamed into a nicely landscaped yard and it suited her and the lovely little house that was hiding behind the trees. Eventually she even redecorated Grandpa's room. But in my heart it's still the Jungle House and to this day whenever I drive or walk through a tunnel of trees I can feel Grandpa with me and I have come to realize that Grandpa wasn't really in the trees of 1233 Hester Avenue. The real magic of Grandpa was that he had put the love for the wild in me. He taught me to do what he had done, to bring what he loved to himself, no matter where he was; and to learn to see what he loved in the world around him no matter what surrounded him.

I have one last image of Grandpa that is my favorite, but I have no photograph to hang on my wall or to share with others. About a year after he died I was still grieving for him, missing him and wishing that some letter or book would show up in the mail with his signature handwriting adorning it; along with multiple layers of packing tape so that you had to use a hacksaw to get into it. I went to sleep thinking of him and I dreamed of Grandpa.

In my dream I sat on the wide, brick steps of his home on Hester Avenue, tying my shoes. The house looked different than I had ever seen it, the whole street did. The trees were young, the landscaping brand new, in fact the whole street seemed young and fresh. I stared up and down the avenue, just waiting for something. Then finally he came, walking down the street; tall, free of pain, braces, and canes, young,

strong and healthy. He smiled at me, put his hands on his hips and said "Come with me!"

Together we walked without speaking through what I recognized was the San Jose that he fell in love with. We walked down neat and tidy city streets where women hung out clean laundry on clothes lines while their husbands tended lemon trees; we walked down dusty country lanes where grass grew between the tire tracks and white fences kept grazing cattle out of blossoming apricot and plum trees. We walked past orchards laden with ripe cherries and fields where children climbed trees and swam in ponds; we walked up the foot hills on the East side and looked out over the valley, all the way to the sea. We walked down again through meadows of tall grasses and wildflowers, beneath canopied halls of old oaks until we stood on a boardwalk beside a silent calliope and small Ferris wheel. We stood in silence looking out over the waves rolling in and out in their endless cycle. At last he turned to me and said "I'm all right, Vernie Lynn, you don't have to worry about me anymore." And in my heart I knew it was true. I looked at him and thought, "If this is your Heaven Grandpa, I can live with it." He seemed to know my mind because he smiled and wrapped his arm around my shoulders and together we stood, watching the rhythm of the sea, the earth, and the sky.

Yes I know he is "all right," and when I stand on the seashore, I still feel that peace, and when I stand under a bower of trees, I still feel his joy in living, and when I look into his eyes in old photographs, I remember to hold onto those I love, to live life fully, and to be unafraid to make choices that move me just a little further down the road of "becoming."

Part Two

Seedlings

Lake Moyie, British Columbia

Principle #12: I am, therefore I do, and what I do makes me who I am

I experienced my first brush with puppy love at the tender age of six. The object of my affection was a sandy-haired boy whose name I don't remember. He told me he liked my pigtails; I told him I wanted to get married, live in a two-story white farm house with a picket fence, a stained-glass front door, and have Bumbleberry flatware and blue willow china.

The miscommunication between the sexes begins early it seems. But he didn't think my demands were too extreme, we agreed to wed and sealed the deal with a kiss at the top of the jungle gym after which my girlfriends and I dissolved into a fit of giggles and ran off, pigtails flying, to plan the upcoming nuptials. It's a sweet, innocent memory.

The summer I turned eight was the year of our first cross-country trek and the year I made up my mind about the kind of man I would marry.

We drove into Oregon—Mom, Dad, Kris, Aaron, Jared, me, and Penny the borrowed Chihuahua—to visit my brother Christer and his family. His kids were always more like cousins than nephews and nieces. We loved spending time with them. After visiting we wound our way through the Willamette Valley, crossed the mighty Columbia River, visited Washington's Grand Coulee Dam and had our last tree-ripened peach confiscated by the Canadian border guard on

our way into British Columbia. My Mom was thoroughly disgusted when she looked back and saw him munching on it as he stopped the next car. In fact, she was so irritated by it that when we left Canada a few weeks later she made Dad stop about ten miles shy of the border so we could eat the last of our Alberta Silver Queen sweet corn before another border guard could swipe it on our way back into the States. We ate so much we could have rolled down into Montana without the wheels on the motor home. To this day I fret about bringing anything edible with me whenever I cross into California. My friend Symbria told me, "Nobody is going to take your grapes, Vernie. Just lie, everybody else does." I'm just such a horrible liar though; I tense up and look guilty, even if it is over a bunch of Red Flame Seedless. I'd probably end up initiating a pat down and car search, spend 6 hours in an interrogation cell, and walk out without a shred of dignity...or my grapes.

In spite of the thieving border guard I loved Canada. It reminded me of the mountains of home only bigger, wilder, and denser. The pine trees went on forever, and I had never seen a highway with a designated bike lane before. I was very impressed by that and began to have ideas about a cross-Canadian bike trip until we crossed the Canadian Rockies; after which I gave up the idea altogether. Jared, who (inexplicably to my mind) loved math problems, worked out all of the kilometer to mile conversions for Dad until we pulled into the Lake Moyie, Canadian Provincial Park. State and national parks were our preferred camping areas. We hardly ever stayed in an RV park except when we went through a city or area where no campgrounds were available. And Mom and Dad always seemed to stop early enough in the day to participate in the nightly park activities put on by rangers, park employees, forestry officials, and in the case of Lake Moyie, a Royal Canadian Mounted Police Officer.

I had never seen a Mountie up close before. I think I watched an episode of Dudley-Do-Right once at Grandma Stratton's house, but they were not something I thought about at all until we sat there in the rustic amphitheatre and listened to him speak. He was a young man, probably in his

mid-twenties, with dark hair and a friendly smile. He spoke to us about the history of the park, pointing out the differences in tree species and the kinds of animals we could expect to see along the hiking trails in the area. He smiled at me with his handsome mouth, his dark hair tidy and neat under his wide-brimmed hat, his smart red uniform standing out in the gathering dusk.

I was completely smitten.

I can hardly be blamed for it though; after all he was a tall, dark, handsome officer of the law on a horse. What girl wouldn't fall in love? He became the quiet ideal of what I was looking for in a young man. He was fit, carried himself surely, and he knew all about trees. I never did find slouchy, slovenly boys at all attractive after that. I could never see what my friends found appealing in the boys who didn't know how to operate a hairbrush, shuffled their feet when they walked, and acted like they had no greater interest in life than to waste time. Who'd want to tie themselves to that? I had friends who drooled over men who wore their hair long and permed, their faces painted with heavy guy-liner. They always made me think of drag queens though most drag queens looked a lot better.

It's interesting to look back at the kind of man I expected to marry at eight and recognize the influence of that subtle decision. It's fascinating because at eight my decision was not based on peer pressure, hormones, fads, or popularity. It wasn't even based on a selfish desire for picket fences and stained glass. My admiration was not a result of what he could do for me or how he would make me look when I was with him; I simply admired him for who he was: a clean, neat, dedicated and knowledgeable defender of right.

I could stop here and go into a discussion of how the appearance of standing up for what's right is not the same as actually doing it. I think everyone has run into that before. If it weren't so common a dilemma, the term "a wolf in sheep's clothing" might not be so well known. But I've noticed a trend

that has been going on, since long before I was born I think, of young men and women who try to appear troubled, delinquent, rebellious, or repressed who then take the higher, more difficult path of doing the "right thing" 50 percent of the time. In this way their mediocrity looks amazing and their approaching status quo looks noble. I can make this observation fairly because I stood among that group for a portion of my young teenage years. Not for long thankfully. I just couldn't wrap my mind around playing the part of a mindless nit-wit part of the time so I could make an intelligent remark later that would resemble a stroke of genius coming from the "airhead." I knew young men who came from homes where they were loved by their parents, given opportunities to learn, grow, and succeed but they thought it looked cooler to act the part of an "outsider" with maladjustment issues. They choose the part they wanted to play, behaving as if life were a stage upon which they could choose the character they wanted to perform, without thought to the consequences of those actions when they decided later to change their lines.

> Every step of our path together has brought us to where we are now, and we have learned the power of forgiveness and new beginnings.

The inherent danger in adopting a false persona is that it often becomes the person. That which we persist in and pursue reflects who we want to become. And who in their right mind wakes up in the morning and says, "I think I'll be morose, depressed, self-absorbed, and miserable today"?

The worst thing about this egotistical malaise afflicting the young and old alike is the compassion and help it draws away from individuals who really are troubled, delinquent, and repressed. It's incredibly selfish and it leaves me wondering...why do we do it?

While philosophers' might still debate Descartes' principle, "I think therefore I am," I'd like to ask "You are

what?" Conscious? Alive? Congratulations on that, we're glad you are. Human? Okay, welcome to the family. I'm not sure it's enough to say "I think therefore I am." I believe it's essential to add, "I am therefore I do." And then to revisit often the question, "What do I do?" "What am I doing that makes me who I am?"

I saw only one tiny speck of that young mounted policeman's life, a mere thirty minutes out of years spent on Earth, but because he chose to do something positive with his time it made an impact on me. That is at the center of why we must "do" in order to "be." Our lives are not lived in solitary confinement and every moment spent on regretting wasted time, lost loves, or poor choices denies us and others the blessing that our lives could be.

I know of youth who waste their time on the frivolous and the vain because they fear they will never truly touch the heart of another human being. I know the elderly who lock themselves away in their rooms dedicated to nothing but memory and physical pain, afraid to offer anything to anyone else because it takes so much energy to simply keep drawing breath each day. I know the infirm who are so wrapped in their own disability and resentment that they have become immune and hateful toward the kindness and service offered by those who love them. I know the busy, middle-aged who fill their days with endless activities so that not a spare moment remains in which to pause, meditate, and reflect on what they might be missing or upon the realization that perhaps all of the "good" they pursue pales next to the "better" which requires less pursuit and more patience.

That young Royal Canadian Mounted Policeman became a portion of my perception of the perfect man, along with bits of my Dad, my brothers, my grandfathers, and other men I admired as a young girl. I'm grateful to say that I found my perfect match in William. He's my fit farmer who walks with purpose, who knows about trees and horses. When I married him I wasn't looking for an officer of the law to keep me in line, or a replacement father, or for someone who only

knew how to have a good time. I was looking for someone who knew himself, someone who knew that he didn't have to be perfect in order to do good works in the world, someone who was willing to do small acts of service with great amounts of dedication and love.

And as it turns out I have my white, two-story farm house anyway. I don't have any stained glass in the front door, but I do have beautiful paintings on my walls. I don't have a picket fence but I have peonies in the spring. I still wish I had Bumbleberry flatware; mine are lousy and need to be replaced. I have green dishes instead of blue, and coordinating chicken-adorned dessert plates. I can look back at the sweet innocence of my first kiss at the top of the jungle gym and my love struck smile in the presence of my RCMP Officer with humor and no regret. I look back on what has been my real love story with all its laughter, tears, tenderness, and hurt with a sense of gratitude and no regrets in spite of moments I am not proud of. Because every step of our path together has brought us to where we are now, and we have learned the power of forgiveness and new beginnings. We have found our strength in living our lives on purpose, in knowing we "are" and choosing to "do" what we believe is right because mediocrity and status quo are not our aim; and we never know from day to day who will come into our life for just a few minutes and the power that time can have upon them and upon ourselves.

Our lives cross over one another's, like ripples on the surface of Lake Moyie where we skipped our rocks. Images and memories fill our minds and our hearts, reflecting back to us the perspective we have chosen. Make your perspective a good one so that the ripples you send out from your choices will be the momentum that lifts another person and not the tide that drags them down and drowns them.

There is power, joy, and peace in knowing ourselves, choosing our path, and defending our truth. And I can say with certainty that having someone to stand beside you makes

it easier to stay upright when the way gets hard, the world cold, and the journey long.

Every day I fall more deeply in love with my husband. I often wonder how I got along without him before we were married and ponder how I would live without him now. But I know that when one of us takes that last leap into the unseen path ahead, the one that separates us for a season, the love that lives in our hearts will keep our companionship alive until we walk together down endless roads, past fertile fields, where no journeys end.

Aunt Sybil

Principle #13: Never forget those who have come before you, honor their lives with your actions

I met Sybil in the summer of 1981 and the thing that I remember most about her is that she was only a few inches taller than I was. Since I was only 7 at the time you can imagine that she was very petite. I had heard about her for years from my Grandpa Stratton. She was his oldest sister and he always spoke of her with such love and respect that I couldn't wait to meet her.

Sybil lived in the town of Big Bend, Wisconsin, in the same house that she was born and raised in. She was born in 1902 and in all that time I don't believe the home changed that much, with the exception of electricity added in the 1920s and indoor plumbing in the 40s. It sat on the edge of a pond that was spring-fed. My Grandpa had a pair of racing skates he had used on that pond hanging over the door to his bedroom all the way out in San Jose, California. Just by virtue of their placement in his room, I knew how important that small pond was to him growing up.

The pond was their playground all through their youth. Grandpa once told me that the great pianist, Liberace, had grown up across the pond from him. It made my grandpa sad to remember that he and his friends had often gone to Liberace's home to invite him to play baseball, ice hockey, or other childhood games but he was never allowed to. His

mother would call out "Mind your hands, son!" and he would be left alone with his music and his mother.

As we stood on the banks of that much loved pond in the warmth of the summer sunshine, I imagined a curly red-haired, freckle faced little boy streaking across the top of its frozen surface.

Sybil walked to the edge of the water and cast some feed out on the surface. Within seconds a small flock of ducks swam up to eat and waddled up to the feet of my great-aunt. She cooed at them and petted their glossy feathers while they waggled their bodies, almost like a puppy, in delight at her touch.

I'm not sure if my parents purposely planned our trip to Big Bend to coincide with the annual 4th of July celebration, but we were there during the classic midwestern festivities. It was a wonderful celebration of not only American history, but also the history of the town. Sybil in particular was being honored. As the city historian she had taught the local and state history to the 3rd and 4th graders at Big Bend Elementary for over 30 years. She had also volunteered her time at the local history and genealogical museum for decades.

So in honor of this service and dedication she had provided so lovingly to her community, they voted in favor of honoring her in the 4th of July parade, and because of her donation of treasured family heirlooms they were able to build and host a grand opening for the "Sibyl Yug Memorial Museum."

It was wonderful to stand on the hot sidewalk in that little Wisconsin town, my hands and pockets full of salt-water taffy, Dum-Dum's, and Tootsie Rolls thrown from the floats and wave like mad at a tiny little woman riding in the back of a great-big car, whom I had met only the day before but because of our shared history had come to love. My love for her was instantaneous. My grandparents and parents had

prepared my heart with stories of her so that when we met it was easy to fall in love with the little woman with the big heart.

I was thrilled to stand there in that humid July heat and know that I was a part of that little community. It was my family history happening right in front of me.

We left Sybil and her home by the pond a short time later, with hugs and kisses and smiles on our faces. That is the memory I like best of her: a sweet woman standing by a small house under a huge tree, waving with a smile on her face.

If life were a movie set and I were the producer, this is the final scene when I would yell "Cut!" and I could walk away from the characters believing that all endings are "happily ever after." If this were a work of fiction I could end the story here, but it is not fiction, and that is not the end of Sybil's story.

> More important to me than past fame and glory
> were the enfolding arms
> of my grandpa's oldest sister around my shoulders,
> and the gentle hands of my mother
> on the frail feet of a stranger.

Two years later in the fall of 1983 we went to visit Sybil again. I was expecting to see the leaves of her giant tree turning with the cooler weather and drifting lazily down to float and rock on the water of the pond. But Sybil no longer lived in her childhood home by the edge of the pond. She was on the second story of a large building in town.

I didn't know what the building was, it looked like a hospital, but I hadn't heard my parents say that Sybil was ill. I had only been to a hospital when someone I knew was sick. They weren't happy places.

I had never even heard the term "rest home" before our visit, but I soon learned the name. That is what the two

story building was. It may not have been a hospital, but it was not a happy place either.

As we walked through the halls I could smell the underlying fragrance of bodily waste and despair. My mother, normally an extremely happy woman was subdued and seemed sad.

We found Sybil in a small dark room; her tiny frame that two years earlier had seemed petite but strong was now frail and wasted. She was so glad to see us, but it was so hard to see her.

There were only a few pictures on the wall to mark the tremendous impact her life had been on her family and community. She sat alone in a small, sterile room with only her memories to surround her. We stayed as long as we could, visiting about family members and what was happening in their lives. She smiled and held my mother's hand the entire time.

As we left I saw my mother wipe her eyes, shake her head and murmur something to my Dad. I don't remember what they said to one another as I wasn't listening to their words. But I do remember what I saw next.

As we neared the exit of the rest home my Mom slowed down as she passed an elderly woman hunched over in a wheelchair. Several nurses passed by us but only my Mom stopped and looked back at the woman. She was leaning over, trying to reach her slippers which had come off of her feet, but she couldn't touch them no matter how hard she tried. My Mom walked back to her and knelt down. She took the woman's feet in her hands and cried "Oh, your feet are so cold!" Then she placed the slippers back on her feet and helped her to sit back up in her chair.

I'll never forget that woman's face. She looked up at my mother with tears in her eyes, her lower lip quivering and grabbed her hand. Mom ran her hand over the soft white hair on the woman's head and leaned down to give her a kiss. I

132

don't think she spoke, and I don't remember anything else from that day, but I've thought of those scenes often over the years.

The thoughts of Sybil make me sad. It hurts to think of the bright, generous woman once honored by her community and so casually forgotten. What good is a name on a building when that name is absent from the hearts of those who built it? I remember the parade with waves and cheers, and I remember a lonely cheerless room in a prison for the elderly.

And then I remember my mother's tears. They weren't tears for lost glory or family pride, they were tears of compassion for a woman she had spent summers with in her teens, for a woman she had taught her children to love. They were tears for a woman she had never met before, whose name she never knew, but who had wept over the simple touch of human kindness. Just like Sybil she had lived her life, been a part of a community, had been a friend, a neighbor, and a teacher; yet there she sat forgotten and alone.

My brother drove through Big Bend recently and stopped in at the little museum. The director was thrilled to see him, more so when he told her who his people were. She showed him charts and told him stories of our family who had been the first settlers in the area. It was exciting to hear. The information sent me searching books and websites to learn more.

But no matter how much I read and learn of our history I still come away feeling that more important to me than past fame and glory were the enfolding arms of my grandpa's oldest sister around my shoulders, and the gentle hands of my mother on the frail feet of a stranger. That, I hope, will be our greatest family legacy. Not just a name on a building, but a warmth in the heart and a strength in the spirit because it isn't just the knowing where we come from that makes us who we are. It's choosing every day to look for a way to teach a child, to touch a heart, or to lift a stranger. It's building in our homes a love of life, family, and friends.

This is the legacy Sybil left.

The Great Stone Mountain

Principle #14: Learn to see the world from more than one perspective

I was sublimely oblivious as a child to just about everything that didn't interest or involve me directly. I hope I'll be forgiven for that, I was a child after all; but somewhere along the second journey my family took around the United States of America that began to change. I'm sure the change in my psyche was due partly to the fact that I was maturing a little (honestly it was probably a very little) as a ten year-old, and partly because of the sheer volume of information and experiences that were being poured through my brain on our extended travel. History, both family and national, was coming to life before my eyes. The vastness of the civilization I belonged to was starting to sink into my cerebrum and notions and certainties I had never questioned suddenly were being brought into the light to be dusted off, visited, explored, and made to explain themselves.

My parents were not seeking entertainment when they set out with us in the 1977 GMC Eleganza II. After all what is remotely entertaining about spending three months in a small space with a noisy ten-year-old girl and two boys, 11 and 12 years old? No, entertainment was not high on their list of priorities, nor were they interested in visiting all the well-worn tourist stops. We left in early September, first to avoid the crowds of summer and second because my Mom wanted to see the fall colors in New England. It might seem odd that

she would have been willing to drive so far just to see some orange leaves, but then if you knew my mother it wouldn't seem odd at all. She is after all her father's daughter, with a deep and abiding love for trees, leaves, and anything that has to do with forests and hills. AND she was the one to inherit (and pass on I might add) her mother's gypsy feet. She loves to travel. Even now she calls from time to time to ask me about motor homes for sale on eBay and she makes plans to travel with Dad and their English bulldog Dozer (short for "Bulldozer") around the country. Her health keeps her from traveling much, but she plans, plots, dreams, marks dates on the calendar, and makes several trips each year to visit family.

So no, it wasn't odd at all to see us heading north on Interstate 5 from Lakehead, California, towards Oregon, Washington, and then the Canadian border and onward and upward to parts unknown in search of colored leaves. When I really think about it I realize I've never left that journey; I still choose to travel out-of-the-way roads just so I can see the trees.

We took with us enough academic work from the local school district to last for months, a boxed set of National Geographic maps given to us by Grandpa Stratton, and a burning desire to see as much of the United States and Canada as we could. We visited dams, state and national parks, British Columbia where I fell in love with an RCMP officer, Mt. Rushmore, the Tetons, the unending grain fields of the American bread basket and eventually down to the southern states where we experienced first-hand the well-known southern hospitality.

The South was a beautiful and foreign place to me. I have never been anywhere so green except maybe northwest Washington State with all its ferns and pines. I was amazed by it. I sat with my nose to the motor home window and drank it in hungrily as we passed mile after mile of ivy, kudzu, and moss covered trees. To a girl raised in the pine needle strewn forests of the southern Cascades and the golden hills of

California covered in their beautiful but dry undulating waves of grasses the south seemed like a verdant oasis.

We visited my brother Kirk who was serving in the Army at Fort Polk, Louisiana, and traveled on across Mississippi, Alabama, and on into Georgia. For some reason we missed Florida; to this day it's one of only three states I haven't been to. Alaska and Hawaii are the other two, and I'm not sure I should really count Rhode Island since we just drove in and then out to say we'd been there.

Georgia provided an opportunity for me to question myself, my understanding of things, my hitherto unwavering view of history and what the term "patriotism" meant. I didn't like it. It's not a comfortable thing to be ten years old and have to question your own thinking, especially when everything you're thinking is a relatively recent understanding to begin with. No, I didn't like it but I am profoundly grateful for the experience I had in Georgia at the Great Stone Mountain.

Geologically speaking Stone Mountain is amazing all by itself. It's a massive piece of solid granite that rises 700 feet into the air. It sits half buried in the earth making you wonder if it's like an iceberg with only ten percent of its mass exposed or if it isn't a weapon once thrown by some giant Titan in a time before time. The height, length, and breadth alone would be impressive but added to that are three huge relief sculptures commissioned by the United Daughters of the Confederacy back in 1916. The men in the sculptures? Jefferson Davis, Robert E. Lee, and Stonewall Jackson.

We arrived at Stone Mountain Park well after the summer crowds had departed. The skating rink was closed as was the miniature golf course, but since I never did learn to skate well and it always took me twenty swings to sink a ball in miniature golf, I didn't mind overly much. The gondola ride to the top of the mountain was still operating and it was a terrifying (since I'm afraid of heights) and thrilling (because I love views from a height) trip up the side of the mountain.

We watched as those larger-than-life, austere, carved faces came ever closer, finally passing them and stepping out on top of the mountain to see a ring of flags from all around the world waving in the warm, sun-washed Georgia air.

My parents wandered the display, reading signs and I was left wondering at the reverence they showed.

I didn't get it.

On a basic and fundamental level I was perplexed. I wanted to raise my hand like a timid student and say, "Um, excuse me but aren't these men…you know…the enemy?"

That's what I thought. I went through the history books in school and that's the knowledge I came away with. Abraham Lincoln and the Northerners were the good guys who believed in freedom and they won because they were "right." Jefferson Davis and the Confederate army were the bad guys because they wanted to destroy the Union, they believed that black men weren't men at all, and the South lost because they were "wrong." That's what my public school version of history had taught me.

That's what I thought and I hadn't known until then that books could be biased or that history could have more than one perspective, one of which could be considered just as correct as the other based on your world view.   I was proud of the fact that I came from "good Yankee stock," as my Grandpa was fond of saying, because we won and we were right. Interestingly, his definition of Yankee and my understanding of the term were two different things. I thought about it in a two tone battle between Blue and Gray. I only thought of the term "Yankee" in relationship to "Rebel." Grandpa saw it as a heritage passed down from before the Revolutionary War when we were all rebels dedicated to personal freedom.

Freedom. It's a powerful word, fraught with meaning and passion and used by people throughout time to promote themselves and their beliefs. But what is it really at the heart

138

of it? What is freedom? Is it synonymous with words like "fair" or "equal?" Is it the antonym of words such as "poverty" and "depravity?" Is it wealth and ease? Is it toil and sacrifice? I have my own definition, I've forged it over the course of my life on Earth and I hope I've learned enough to keep my eyes open to new views of it. My understanding began very young as a student of my parents, learning simple truths from them that revolved around what is good and bad, right and wrong. The moments I stood atop the Great Stone Mountain added another layer to that understanding.

Before I stood there, I only comprehended the Civil War in terms of black and white, bond and free, Blue and Gray. But walking that space, watching my parents treat with respect men I believed chose "wrong," who fought for the side I know our family would have fought against had we lived then, I was forced to view the conflict between states, ideologies, and families in greater depth.

Would these men really have willingly sacrificed their livelihoods, their honor, and their families' security for greed? I had believed that. Greed and laziness, that's what I had learned in school. Could there have been something deeper that drove them? For some I imagine their personal support of the secession and the ensuing war were based on economic gains; profiteering, and pirating. But for some, like the leaders who were carved on the face of the granite upon which I stood, I believe it was something more.

For good or ill I believe that the fight for them was less about slavery and more about the power of personal agency. The irony of this sentiment is not lost on me, how can you claim you believe in agency on one hand and deny it to someone else on the other? But I'm willing to believe the best in people and I believe that the men on the face of that grand mountain of granite were willing to fight to the death for the right to choose for themselves the path they would take, whether the path was correct or not. My parents didn't tolerate greed in themselves or their children and they would not have revered it in leaders of men. But they did revere those men on the mountain.

I have since then read and studied their lives and can agree with my parents that they were indeed honorable men—honest and duty bound to their personal convictions, brave beyond what I understand and, in opposition to what the enormous sculpture would imply, humble. They were not a self-righteous, sanctimonious group. These were men who believed unwaveringly in the right of the people to govern themselves. They recognized that sometimes the people are unwise, but they were humble enough to learn from their mistakes and move forward. I know enough of my own beliefs to know I would have chosen a different path, one that would have followed the Union, President Lincoln, and my ancestors, but I can respect the choice the leaders of the confederacy made even while I don't agree with it.

I'm grateful to my parents for taking us there, for showing me a side to America I had not truly recognized before. I found there on the side of that mountain a new set of heroes to add to my list and another set of beliefs to learn from and understand. It was a powerful lesson for me: to recognize that there are people who I will disagree with politically, morally, and religiously who are just as honorable, dedicated, and principled in their own right and in their own beliefs. I can disagree with their doctrine and their course of action and yet still have respect for their right to choose those actions.

Stone Mountain has become an amusement park now, a destination for fun and frivolity. I hope that while all those families are riding roller coasters, watching laser tag or getting a hole-in-one on the miniature golf greens that they will look up once or twice at the heroes carved on the side of that mountain. I hope that they can see that whether they are black or white, enslaved to debt or free of financial worries, whether they hearken from Mississippi or Maine, that there were men who fought and died so that they could choose for themselves the path they would walk in this life. I hope they feel grateful for both friends and foes past who have brought us to where we are today, that they cherish the gift of freedom, agency, and the power to choose our own paths. And above all I hope they choose well.

Appalachian Wildflowers

Principle #15: Beauty isn't just what we see; it is a way of looking that we share with others

I have always loved my name, Vernie Lynn. As a child I knew that no one else my age had it and there were very few adults who shared it either. It simply isn't a common name and the last time it was well known or popular as a child's name, if it ever was, was during the 1930s. I am named after my father Vern Elliott Johnson (hence the Vern E), as well as my mother's cousin Vernie Belle Stratton, and my mother Janice Lynn. Growing up I was seldom called just "Vernie." I was always "Vernie Lynn" and I still am to most of my family.

I love the fact that I share a name with my Dad. He has been my hero all my life, and I am proud and grateful that he was willing to let me carry on that part of him. When I was very young, I would pour over old photos of him as a young man. He was dressed up in his double-breasted suit, wool coat, and gray felt fedora; I thought he looked like a movie star with his dark hair, dark eyebrows, and though the pictures were black and white, what I knew were his bright blue eyes.

He would pick me up and toss me in the air when he came in from working in the barn or the fields. He would give me a bear hug and a whisker rub while I squealed, then he'd laugh and set me down again. Sometimes in the evenings he'd lay down for a few minutes with his boots still on for one of his 20-minute cat naps. He'd taught himself as a young father to sleep in small doses while he worked three different

jobs just to keep his family fed, clothed, and in a home. I'd crawl up next to him and say "Daddy, can I tell you a story?"

He'd half wake up, readjust his pillow and say groggily, "Mmm, hmm, go ahead."

I'd launch into long and rambling stories about fairies, trains, and toadstool houses while he alternately snored or mumbled appreciative noises. I wasn't very concerned with whether or not he was asleep, but I loved it that he was willing to listen to me.

I mentioned in an earlier love letter that one of my first memories is of riding with my Dad on the old, diesel Massey-Ferguson tractor. It's one of my favorite memories. Another is the time Dad woke me up at three o'clock in the morning to watch a meteor shower with him from the porch of our home in Lakehead, California. We stood out in the cool, early morning August air watching meteors fly past the tops of the dark pine trees. He looked for little ways to give me personal experiences with him and I treasure them.

The trips we took around the United States were due in large part to my father's search for his place. He had started out in the small, coal-mining town of Price, Utah, where his father owned and operated a trucking business. Grandpa moved his lineup of trucks and his family to San Jose, California, in 1943 and there it blossomed and grew. Dad's older brother Russ took over those reins and Dad dreamed of becoming a pharmacist. He never realized that dream, though his son, my brother Ken did. Over the course of 30 years he grew up, married his Swedish sweetheart Birgit, raised a family, lost his wife and one of their daughters Cynthia in a tragic accident on Christmas Day 1968, met, fell in love again, and married my mom Janice in 1970 and continued raising the "yours, mine, and ours" family that he had begun in 1952, worked hard, tried multiple small business endeavors, and found himself leaving his farm, Hillcrest Orchards, still looking for the place that fit him best. He had loved the farm, but with land re-zoning, higher taxes on what was now

"recreational" land and no longer "agricultural," it was wiser to sell and look for a place where he could farm successfully without the hindrance of higher taxes and tourists.

So in a borrowed Winnebago with my Mom, 4 kids, and a Chihuahua we headed east to look for farmland all across the United States. I don't think he had any solid notion of where he wanted to settle, nor did Mom though they leaned pretty heavily towards the New England states, more from a sense of family nostalgia than any logistical farming needs or concerns.

That first trip took us into Canada, across the vast grain fields of Alberta, down through Glacier National Park along the Teton mountain range and into the heart of Yellowstone. We wound our way in a zigzagging pattern across the USA until we ended up on the coast of Maine in a tiny fishing village. From there we followed the Great Lakes around to Niagara Falls. I think the plan had been to go from there to Michigan and up into Canada again but my father woke up one morning after leaving Buffalo, New York, and said, "We need to head back to San Jose right away." He didn't elaborate really except to say that he felt we needed to go back and see Grandpa Johnson.

We didn't meander on the way home. We drove directly to San Jose, straight to Grandma and Grandpa Johnson's front door. Grandpa Ben was a tall man; age hadn't diminished that though he was 83 by then. I remember so little of Grandpa Johnson. Our time together was limited but I remember that his smile was like my Dad's. It was wide and full and lit up his face and made his eyes shine. He raised lemons, roses, and little bantam chickens. He lived through World War I. I have a picture of him standing with several other soldiers in front of his ammunition truck in Germany (he looks just like my brother Aaron), but he never spoke of his time there. He made me a little cradle for my dolls when I was 5 and painted it a happy orange color to match the afghan that Grandma Johnson had crocheted for me. We sat there in

their living room and visited for awhile then drove across town to stay the night with Grandma and Grandpa Stratton.

I wasn't privy to all of my parents' discussions and concerns, but I could tell that Dad was worried about Grandpa Ben. His heart was not as strong as it used to be, and Dad thought maybe he ought to see the doctor. But doctor or no, Grandpa Johnson's heart was done. Within days of our arrival he had a massive heart attack and he was gone.

It amazed me then, though it doesn't surprise me now, that my father was the one to whom his family looked for emotional and spiritual guidance during times of trouble even though he was the youngest child. But wisdom does not always follow age nor does it shun youth, and my Dad has always sought it. It was my father who made the arrangements for the funeral, ensured that everyone was notified, and made certain that someone was with Grandma.

The Johnsons were a pretty dramatic bunch, maybe melodramatic would be a more accurate word, especially Grandma, so my eight-year-old recollections of the viewing before the funeral are of a great deal of sobbing and mourning, and justifiably so, but I had never heard or seen anything like it before. My only previous experience with death had been when my puppy was run over. I had been certain that the only reason he was dead was because he was in the ground. I thought if we brought him out of the grave again, he would breathe and play with us once more. I had him half dug up before it struck me that death didn't work that way and he wasn't coming back to play with me. Grandma was not an easy person, but oh how she loved Grandpa. I don't think she knew then how she could ever live without him, and I didn't know what to think of her all-consuming grief.

But my Dad was calm. I remember standing next to the casket with him, looking in at Grandpa Ben, the kind man who had been skilled at making roses flourish, and thinking that he wouldn't have liked all the sorrow. He looked so at

peace; I know he would have wanted everyone else to feel that way too. Dad was there beside me embodying and emanating that same peace in a living breathing example that I could draw strength from and learn to follow.

He still emanates peace, not because he's mild-mannered (he's not...at all) but because he lives his life the best way he can and in all his decisions he seeks to act in accordance with his convictions, his truths, and to be a good steward over his responsibilities. "Responsibilities" is a word too often lumped with negative terms like "the weight of..." or "too many" or "drowning in..." Responsibilities should be no more and no less than that which is within our sphere of influence that we have the power to improve or make better. It requires a compassionate heart, a clear eye, and a judicious hand because not all improvements are equal and not all betterment looks the same.

It amazes me how often people come to my Dad for advice or to butt heads with him because they want to convince him that they are correct. I've wondered why they do it. There's no earthly reason for it. He's not handing out grant money or diplomas, pay checks, or awards. As far as I can tell, it's simply a matter of respect. They respect his opinion; it matters to them even when they disagree. The funny thing about my Dad is he won't agree with anyone who is incorrect just to make them feel better. He believes, as I do, that living a life of correctness, which is to say living a life that is in harmony with that which you value, is the path to happiness. It's impossible to work against what you value and find any lasting peace. And so when people come to him, as they always do, with questions or complaints or arguments, he will usually challenge them to live up to what they believe. It's phenomenal how many of them want him to change his beliefs to make them feel better. It wouldn't work, of course, because it's not what he believes that bothers them anyway; it's the belief in their own heart that hammers away at them, a slow and steady beat that reminds them continually of who they really are, or who they can really become.

I think perhaps in part that was what Dad was looking for in his trek across America and back again—the place where he best fit, the place where he could be his best self. He told me once, years after our two cross-country adventures, that "It doesn't really matter where you finally decide to settle down. It's that you choose your place and do everything you can in your place to serve others."

We settled for a time in Lakehead, California, but we knew from the start that it wasn't the last stop. We talked and laughed over all the options open to us as a family. We never dreamed small. After all if you're going to dream, why be dinky about it? One week it was a dairy in Wisconsin, the

 next it was a lobster boat off the coast of Maine, then it was a grove of maple trees in Vermont, or a field of corn in Iowa. Our family dreams all centered around agriculture of some sort. I don't think Mom and Dad ever considered going back to the city. When we dreamed it was always of acres, crops, and dirt under our nails. My parents had found such peace on the farm I don't think they could ever go back to the hustle and frenetic energy of the city life. Their hearts were more in tune with the

energy of growing, of the slow and steady, eternal progression of season, seed, and harvest.

We set out the second time from Lakehead in our own motor home, the much loved GMC, to see America and catch a glimpse of what made her great. It was that trip that truly changed my life, my perspectives, and added an element to my own foundation that has rooted my personal core values to the soil and to the worth, divinity, and power of the human soul.

So many memories of that trip fill my mind at odd moments, it can be difficult 27 years after the fact to look back and separate them all: watching fireflies in the Ozarks, standing in a simple grove of trees that changed the life of an ancestor, finding unknown cousins in a tiny Alberta town, honoring fallen heroes and living ones. And yet the one that I remember the most often, the one that comes to me in quiet moments when I am traveling down back country lanes that I inevitably seek out to drive down and speaks the loudest to me of who Dad was and is and what he has passed on to me, happened on a narrow strip of road, carved out as a view area along the Blue Ridge Parkway in North Carolina. We stopped at a lot of those. We stopped at view areas, overlooks, and tiny history markers. We traveled down two-lane highways and visited the local museums of small-town America; thus, it was not a surprise to find ourselves standing at the edge of the asphalt looking out over the Blue Ridge Mountains just beginning to burst with colors in late September. The fragrance of wood smoke and mist clung to the branches and leaves of the hollows, clouds slid lazily across a cool, blue autumn sky, and black oiled gravel crunched under our feet as we peered down the edge of the hillside on which we stood. My father isn't one for talking much; he says few words and he chooses them with care. Sometimes it's a well-spoken word of humor, comfort, or guidance. He didn't speak as we stood there, and in the silence my eyes and feet wandered to a group of long-stemmed wildflowers that were blooming at the edge of the road. I didn't know then that they were rudebeckia, echinacea, and chicory. I thought they were

149

lovely and in the way of young girls I bent down to pick them. I'm sure my father was accustomed to me picking flowers, goodness knows I brought my share of dandelions into the house, and he didn't mind a bit but this time e stopped me.

"Let them grow Vernie Lynn," he said. "Just look at how hard they've worked to thrive where they are. They've survived being buried in asphalt, they've survived all the exhaust that tries to choke them and they even survived the mowers. Let's let them grow for someone else to see."

I pulled my hand back from their stems. I hadn't known that Dad noticed wildflowers growing by roadsides. I noticed them all the time and in my joy in their beauty I'd been willing to pluck them up to show them to everyone. Dad taught me another way. He taught me that sometimes beauty exists because of the place and our relationship to it. The wildflowers by the roadside were beautiful because they were by the roadside; beautiful alone yes, but more so because of the beauty they shared with what was around them.

We left them there, an array of purple, yellow, and pink simplicity on the side of a Carolina highway, blooming in the place they had found, the place they had decided to stay and make beautiful. I think of them from time to time and hope that the seeds from those blossoms have flourished, multiplied, and beautified their bit of earth.

My father finally found his place, his fields, in northwestern Missouri. He has tended them well, as good a steward of the land as I have ever seen. Mom called me just a week or so ago to tell me they are turning all of their fields back into pasture this year. It has produced grain for nearly a decade and it's time for it to rest. She told me that Dad will be planting 50 acres of something else this year, something I hadn't expected but which shouldn't surprise me: wildflowers.

I believe with all my heart that with such a gardener as my father to tend them, they can't help but grow.

Seaside Markets and Roadside Stands

Principle #16: Go in search of the greatest American Principle:
Gratitude

I've shared in other love letters my Mother's love for the beauty of the American countryside and her desire to see it dressed in all its glowing fall finery. But it wasn't just the trees arrayed in their bright autumn ball gowns that she longed to see. It was the multi-sensory experience of the country at harvest time that she wanted for all of us to see, hear, feel, smell, and taste. While Dad stopped at all the history markers on the two lane highways that crisscrossed the U.S., Mom aimed us towards all of the farm stands, apple shanties, and fruit filled wheelbarrows that bore examples of the diligence and skill of small-scale American farmers. We ate Oregon blackberries, white Alberta sweet corn, Gulf Coast prawns the size of my hand, fresh from the sea in Louisiana, pecan pies made from freshly picked nuts and centuries old recipes in Georgia, freshly pressed Concord grape juice in Pennsylvania, and ripe, musky apples along the banks of Lake Champlain, New York.

Whenever possible my Mom bought local produce for our meals. She loved the higher quality of freshly harvested vegetables and fruits. She knew what quality looked like, felt like, and smelled like. She had learned to select the best at her father's side in the pre-war markets in San Jose, California, when farm goods would be delivered to local grocers every morning, the dirt still moist on their roots. I watched her pick

up bunches of juicy Muscat grapes and select the one that was the fullest. She picked through the Thompson seedless bunches until she found the vine that held the most sun-freckled and sweetest grapes. She exclaimed over apple varieties that hadn't grown in our heirloom orchard. We sampled fruit with crimson skin and snowy white flesh and some with mottled yellow-orange and green on the outside and rose and ivory on the inside. How delicious they were! Crispy, sweet, and juicy. We found bottles of icy cold, fresh pressed, and un-pasteurized apple cider. We hadn't tasted anything that good since we'd left Montgomery Creek and our own ranch nearly three years earlier.

We stopped at a wonderful roadside market in Vermont, the wooden porch of the little red building adorned with fat, cheery pumpkins and golden shocks of corn. Inside were a multitude of maple inspired gifts and confections. My Mom bought little leaf shaped candies from the clerk and handed one to each of us. I held it in the palm of my hand, saw the lovely sugar sculpted leaf veins and thought they were too pretty to eat. But when I placed that maple sugar candy on my tongue and felt the sandy-sweet flavor dissolve in my mouth, it was more than flavor that I tasted. It was clean as a hard-wood forest, as rich as a field of clover, and as filling as a grandmother's kitchen. That is the joy of good food. It's so much more than the sensation on the tongue. It's as if our taste buds have access to the memories of all the ingredients, and they fill the heart of the eater as well as the stomach.

We nibbled our way through states and tastes experiencing the history of America and her yearly harvests. We ended up on the coast of Maine in a small seaside village that overlooked the Atlantic, in front of a restaurant that boasted freshly caught lobster for dinner. My Mom has always loved seafood and she taught the rest of us to love it too so she and Dad decided to treat each of us to a lobster of our own.

It was an experience I will not soon forget; indeed nearly 30 years later I can still remember it clearly. There we

were, seated around a table in an obviously upscale restaurant, preparing to eat what most people consider to be a delicacy. The waiters came out with huge platters laden with plates covered in bright red, shiny shelled crustaceans.

I stared at my lobster.

It stared back at me with beady, black, hard-boiled eyes and evil looking claws.

I blurted out (quite loudly I might add), "Eww! It looks like a beetle!"

The waiter looked shocked and somewhat taken aback by my pronouncement. There was an awkward pause and silence in the restaurant for about 4 seconds, and then the whole establishment broke out into laughter. The waiter smiled at me and nodded. He said "Yes it does, but it tastes delicious!" He was right; it did.

> If we travel across the country so that we can sit in a hotel room, watch pay-per-view, and eat delivery pizza ...did we really go anywhere?

For almost every destination we went to I have some kind of association to it with food. I love having my memories of traveling mixed up with my memories of glorious tastes, textures, and nuances of local cuisine. I'm grateful to my Mom and Dad for teaching me to really savor where I was. Too often we travel to a destination to see the sights and deny ourselves the pleasure of feasting on all the "else" it has to offer. We remain outsiders, tourists, passers-by just skirting the edges of experience instead of diving in and knowing a people, place, and culture more fully.

I visited the coast of Oregon just a matter of weeks ago. I sat in a little crab shack, half a step up from a dive, eating fresh fish and chips and watching the locals come and go, striking up conversations on how the high school ball game turned out, the poor catch that day while out on the boats,

153

and the pleasant late summer weather. The food was amazing. They had smoked salmon candy bites that I'm already looking forward to sharing with William when we visit again. I drove through town on my way back to my hotel and saw license plates from Delaware, Iowa, and Saskatchewan lined up in the fast food drive-through lane. "What a shame" I thought. It's a shame to travel all the way across the continent just so you can eat the same food you could have had just across the street at home. It's a shame to visit a place you've always wanted to see and close yourself off to everything you can touch, taste, smell, and feel there too.

How can you really experience the power of the sea if you never stand on the shore and feel the waves erode the sand from beneath your toes or the sense of vertigo that pulls you towards its immenseness? How can you really experience the majesty of the mountains if you never try to scale a part of it and struggle against the wind just to stay standing? How can you fully appreciate the labor of love it takes to keep the American people fed until you stand at the edge of a field and watch a green-black hailstorm move towards you like a giant, water hued, devouring fire, knocking down thousands of acres of corn, wheat, oats, and soybeans along its path to self-destruction?

We too often close ourselves off from experiencing and doing good works because of our fear of the different and the unknown. We are too accustomed to having our whims and wishes satisfied in an instant with no real effort on our part. After all, why visit the Grand Canyon if you can just watch a documentary of it on television? Why settle for one slice of really good pizza when you can get a poor quality but super-sized one for five bucks? If a tiny amount of high quality is good then a huge portion of mediocre or crummy should make up the difference...right? Why get our hands messy at a local food pantry or community garden that has planted a "row for the hungry" when we can just press the $1.00 donation button as we check out at the grocery store and the screen asks "Would you like to donate to (insert the charity of your choice) today?" It requires no effort on our part and it

makes me wonder: If our modern society has made service so easy that all it requires from us is that we toss a few pennies at it and no sacrifice at all...is it really service? If we travel across the country so that we can sit in a hotel room, watch pay-per-view, and eat delivery pizza...did we really go anywhere?

It's all symptomatic of the same diseases: Adrenaline Junkie Apathy and American Cultural Deficiency Disorder.

I went to the Oregon State fair with my family a little over a month and a half ago. They had some of the same old rides I remember from my childhood; the Tilt-a-Whirl, Spider, and the Haunted Fun House. Then they had this thing that I can only describe as a giant sling-shot that shot a couple of lunatics at a time 100 feet in the air where they could flip around, scream, and potentially pee their pants. Don't misunderstand me, a little adrenaline is okay. I enjoy roller coasters and fast airplane take-offs. But the bigger, better, faster, and scarier atmosphere that pervades our movies, music, and other entertainment has desensitized us and especially our children to the beauty, depth, and emotional thrill of leaves in the fall, the smell of wood smoke on a winter eventide, and the wonder of wildflowers in a spring drenched Rocky Mountain meadow. When we become addicted to the next adrenaline high from a ride, a game, a drink, or a fast car, we can't ever get enough and we start to live in fear of the lows.

Quiet is our enemy; calm becomes our foe.

The adrenaline junkie suffers from an appalling sense of apathy concerning the beauty and wonder of the world around him. I saw it in the eyes of some of the youth at the shore who glanced up, glassy-eyed, from their Nintendos to stare at the ocean as if it were a blank screen. It's almost a horror movie plot in and of itself to think of those young people living "virtual" lives, never noticing that the real thing is slowly passing them by.

Our American culture is eroding with every family that chooses to spend their vacation watching another family live a "real-life." We are losing the legacy of our boot-strap pioneers and forefathers in the face of an ever-increasing self-absorption geared toward ease and entitlement. We have lost our open-armed hospitality of Emma Lazarus's "Colossus" that cried "Give me your tired, your poor, your huddled masses yearning to breathe free;" in the face of a self-fulfilling plague of scarcity. We live in a land of abundance and drown in our debt and our debris of "more."

More food, more money, more clothes, more cars, more toys, more appliances, more media, more concrete, more houses, more electric wires, more competition, more, more, more.

What have we paid for it with?

Silence.

Simplicity.

Order.

Peace.

We are losing our culture very simply because we don't know what it means to be American anymore. Is America defined by race? I don't believe so. I'm Caucasian, my sister-in-law is Oriental, but we're both American. Is America defined by ethnic heritage? I'm a Scots-English-Irish mix. My husband is French with some Swiss mixed in. Half my siblings are Swedish. My nieces are Korean yet we're all Americans. Is America defined by how long you've lived in the country? My ancestors came over in the 1620's; their descendants fought in the revolutionary war. Three of my brothers and sisters are first generation Americans; but they are Americans.

I believe that the power, grandeur, humility, and responsibility that makes up and defines what America is and

what American culture can be is found in one simple word: Gratitude.

Gratitude for the chance to worship freely, work honestly, and to build responsibly. Gratitude for the right to try and fail and try again. Gratitude for the right to speak your mind and vote your conscious without fear. Gratitude for the chance to be forgiven of past wrongs, to offer redress and try harder next time. Gratitude for the weight, responsibility, and sacrifice it requires to keep a democratic republic strong. Gratitude for the restraints of courtesy that allow someone you disagree with to express their view with dignity and offer you the chance to dispute with truth but not acrimony.

Gratitude is what invites us to our knees and lifts us to our feet in prayers and anthems. Gratitude is what pushes us past our own front door to see the poverty at someone else's and reach out a hand in generosity. Gratitude is what allows us to open our hearts to those that fear and our hands to those who long for understanding and compassion. It is gratitude that is the cornerstone of our American culture. Not rebellion, dissidence, anger, or arrogance.

But we cannot feel gratitude when we are caught in an apathetic stupor. We cannot see anything to be grateful for when our minds are numbed by the anesthesia of indifference. To really feel gratitude requires sacrifice. To really sacrifice we must seek out a way to serve. To find a way to serve requires that we engage all five of our senses. We must look around us at the real people in our own neighborhoods. We must listen for the almost silent pleas that people make daily for a smile, a thoughtful word, or a single touch of human kindness. We must breathe in the fragrance of poverty and despair and feel the texture of its roughness with our own hands so that we can do all in our power to change it. We need to taste the difference between thriving and surviving, or we will disappear like the Mayans or the Aztecs. Future generations will know we were here, but nothing of our greatness will remain.

I can say with conviction that I am grateful for America because I have tasted her sweetness on my tongue. Just as that one piece of maple sugar candy was enough to make me remember it for life so my experiences as a child have been enough for me to know that America is still great. There is such goodness, charity, compassion, and higher purpose in the hearts of her people that the only thing capable of restraining her from doing more good works in the world are our individual fears.

We must learn to see the good in others. We must learn to listen with our hearts to the pleas of other nations and peoples that we may respond with greater understanding and restraint. We must feel more acutely the hunger of our own poor and the poor of other nations and let the smell of carnage and defeat fill our nostrils that we may no more set ourselves apart from those who plead for our aid.   We can start today with something as simple as experiencing the flavors of our own heritage. When was the last time you sat down to a meal with your family? Sit with them. Express gratitude for who they are and who they can be.

If we return our purchases of amusement and entertainment, we may find that we have enough left to buy back our birthright of effort, sacrifice, generosity, and freedom. It might not seem like a fair trade-in until you stand on the shore and feel the sea erode the sand from beneath your toes or until you stand beneath a shower of aspen leaves on the top of a mountain or until you sit on a rough hewn wooden porch, surrounded by pumpkins and Indian corn and feel the sweetness of homegrown maple sugar dissolve on your tongue and experience the collective memory of work and wonder, service and satisfaction for yourself.

This is the America my parents showed me, and it's still there. Maybe it's time to turn off the television, get out the map, and plan a road trip.

Part Three

Fruiting Wood

Leaving the Land

Principle #17: In order to become who we want to be we must give up who we have been

Mid-Summer 2007

I stepped out of my little farmhouse into the warm, balmy summer morning. The sun was still below the horizon, but tiny fingers of golden-rose light were creeping their way across the fields, just barely gilding the edges of the Chinese wisteria draping itself in a mass of green foliage around my porch rails. I looked to the south and could see the early morning fog settled on the top of the pond, the hazy green hills, and the giant rounds of hay bales in the fields. To my left, hidden from those first rays of eastern sunlight by our little garage, my daylilies were just opening their happy orange faces. I couldn't look to the west yet. I knew I would be headed in that direction for the next two days, and I just couldn't do it. So I walked to the edge of the lawn and stood on the little dirt road that passed in front of our house and looked to the north. There stood the culmination of all my hopes and dreams, wishes and wants.

"The Perfect Farm." From the first time I had seen it, I had yearned for it. For a small season I had gloried in possessing it, and now in spite of all the tears, after all my pleadings and frustrations, I was saying goodbye.

The Big Red Barn stood back and to the left of the little white farmhouse. It had housed cows, pigs, horses, mules, and chickens. I loved that barn. It had stood there for

161

a century protecting animals, providing a place for children to play, and standing watch over the men and women who had come to work the soil. The ash tree draped its long, lush branches behind me, and I just wanted to wallow in it. I wanted to sink into the greenness of the land around me and soak it in one last time. Finally, with a heavy heart I turned to the west. The moving truck stood there, packed and ready. The truck and trailer I would be driving stood parked behind it. We would be piling our children in and leaving in just a short time, so little time it seemed. There was no more time to climb the three-story treehouse my husband had built, no more time to climb to the hayloft and play, no more time to gently twist the wisteria and train it the way I wanted. I had run out of time. I felt like Dorothy in the Witch's castle. My sands had run out and a part of me that I loved, probably loved too much, was dying. I didn't cry. There didn't seem to be any point. But the tears burned; all the way down in my soul they burned.

> If you stand out in the field long enough, and stand quiet, you come to understand that it's a living, breathing thing. You put your mark on the soil with your labor, and the soil puts its mark in your heart. I can't get the soil out of my heart.

It seems I am forever leaving the farm. No matter how hard I dig in my heels and fight and hold on by my fingernails, I am still torn away from the land. It's a hard loss to explain to anyone who doesn't have a deep love for the land. They just cluck their tongue and say, "Oh, that's too bad," and just tell you you'll find another piece of property. How can you explain it? It's not just a piece of real estate. It's not just a bunch of surveyor's marks on an abstract. If you stand out in the field long enough, and stand quiet, you come to understand that it's a living, breathing thing. You put your mark on the soil with your labor, and the soil puts its mark in your heart. I can't get the soil out of my heart. I can shake it from my shoes. I can wash it out from under my fingernails, but it is so closely entwined with my soul that I can't get it out.

I don't want to get it out, and it's like losing a limb every time I have to leave it.

It was not the first time I had left a farm; I can only hope that it will be the last.

Mid-March 2010

I penned those thoughts a little over two years ago. It's interesting to me how our lives change and circle back around. How sometimes the things we desire most are the things we have to let go of in order to have what we need the most. Our journey through the last year has been like a camping trip in the Henry Mountains, rough and rocky, worn, devastated but unconquered, and unimaginably beautiful. I wouldn't trade the time we've spent, the friends we have made, or the lessons we've learned for anything.

It has now been almost 2 weeks since we drove away from Paradox, Colorado on a cold but clear March morning. Two moving trucks filled with greenhouses and everything we deemed necessary to setting up a home in the Willamette Valley were parked in the frozen red mud of the yard. A Suburban and trailer and one small, beat-up mini-van were loaded with kids and ready to roll away. William and I and two of our best friends in the world, Mark and Michaela Larsen, stood together and looked around to see if there was anything we had forgotten. We prayed for a safe trip, wished each other luck, checked to make sure we all had each other's phone numbers, and climbed into our respective vehicles. I was to drive point on the trip. So with Ephraim in the front seat beside me and Esther Marilla Joy in her car seat in the back, I set out down the long, red driveway to the highway.

I thought I was ready to leave.

I thought I had the need for leaving balanced with the opportunity of going in my heart. I thought I was prepared to say good-bye.

But somewhere along the first turn of the winding road out of Paradox, I heard a small sound and turned my head enough to see my precious little Marilla looking out the window with tears streaming down her face.

"Baby girl," I called out to her. "What's wrong?"

Her silent tears turned into full on sobs then as she cried out with all the anguish her little 5-year-old heart could muster "I miss Paradox!"

"Oh baby, I know," I told her. "But it's going to be okay. I miss Paradox too. It's okay to cry when you love something; it's okay to be sad when you have to leave. Just remember that we're going to a beautiful place. We'll have a chance to meet new friends, see new things, and we'll still have our Paradox friends."

"But I miss Grandma Hayes!" She wailed and started to cry harder. It tore at my heart and I started to cry too, I didn't even try to hold it in check. I drove as slow as I could so that we could all look at the valley one more time. "I miss Miss Rosie!" The golden light of the sun was just creeping along the fields. I heard another sob and looked over to see Ephraim wiping his eyes on his sleeve. He turned to me, eyes drenched and in all sincerity said, "Now I know how those Oregon Trail pioneers felt when they had to leave their homes."

I admit I lost it then and there. What a sight we must have been; all of us crying our eyes out, telling each other all the things we loved and would miss about Paradox. "I want to tell Diane that she's the best Sunday school teacher I ever had," Ephraim sobbed. "I want to tell Wayne thank you for the belt buckle." Marilla was in the back listing all of her "grandmas" who had adopted her. "I want Grandma Ellie. I miss Grandma Steele. I love Grandma Redd. I forgot to hug Linda goodbye!"

We passed Miss Rosie on the road just after we drove through the cut in the mountain and made our way around

the first turn towards La Sal Creek canyon. I tried to wave while I was wiping my eyes; I hope she saw the wave. We waved at Mark and Amy's house, I don't think they were home at the time, but we thought of our friends as we drove past, and wished we would be there to help with spring pruning on their fruit trees.

I really thought that leaving Paradox would be easier than leaving our Perfect Farm in Missouri. After all, we didn't own the farm or the house where we lived and labored. That should make it easier, right? It wasn't any easier. It was just as hard, just as heartbreaking, and just as necessary as the first move. It's just so ironic that in order to move forward to your biggest goals, your best potential, your greatest success, you have to be willing to let go of who, where, and what you are now.

I guess I know a little bit about how those Oregon Trail pioneers felt too. I loved Paradox. I was so ready to find "home" the first time I drove into that beautiful little valley, and there it was all spread out in green fields and towering red rocks. It felt like home. Even my son Enoch who had asked every week since we left Maryville, Missouri, "When are we going home, Mom?" said as we drove along the grass covered roads, "This place feels like home!"

It did feel like home, and we made it home for almost a year. We were prepared to stay forever and we had sunk our roots down fast and deep. I don't think I've lived anywhere else where the people understood the terms "neighbor" and "community" so well. I've never been as cared for by my neighbors as I was in Paradox. They were so full of love, generosity, and welcome it was staggering. I've heard from several people that they don't think Paradox will ever recover from the political unrest brought on by disagreements over the proposed uranium mill. I disagree completely. The people of Paradox are good neighbors because they choose to be. They don't let a disagreement over politics keep them from gathering together to work, worship, play, or serve. They are a tough breed of people,

dedicated to making their community thrive no matter what. I love them and I wish we could have stayed longer. I admire them, and I hope I can learn from their strength of will and character. But mostly, right now in the "wee small hours of the morning" I simply miss them. I miss their smiles, the surly way of speaking some of them had, the warm embraces of friends, and the simple joy they brought into my life. I couldn't stay in Paradox, but what I learned there will be in my heart forever. I hope that I can take what I learned and be a better friend and a better neighbor where ever I may go in the future.

I've reached the end of my Oregon Trail, but at this point in my journey I don't know if it's the end of my travels or not. But I do know this: no matter where your travels take you, plant your roots deep, hold nothing back in your relationships, BE the good neighbor, give everything you have to offer freely, serve without recompense, and love without fear. You'll find an abundance of friendship, support, and love in return. This is living in Joy: to give everything you have away to receive everything you've ever wanted.

And isn't that a paradox?

Comfort, Courage, and Crop Failure

Principle #18: Be courageous in pursing what you believe in

William and I had been married for about two years when we put our first production size greenhouse into operation. It wasn't a huge frame, measuring only 22x48 feet, just over 1,000 square feet of growing space. We were renting a small one bedroom farmhouse, just up the road from William's parents farm at the time though they were not in residence. My brother Roger, his wife Joy and their eight (yeah I said 8!) children were renting the house while they looked for a place of their own in Missouri.

It was a nice set-up, the greenhouse stood about 100 yards north of the DeMille farmhouse, a smaller propagation hut stood right next to it, and we had been lucky enough to come across an old long-wood furnace which produced heat on a dual fuel system and was set in a small shed directly to the west of the greenhouse. We had a well cared for wood-lot, so heating was easy and the tomato plants that filled the propagation house were tall, lush, and almost ready to be planted into the beds prepared for them in the larger house. Now, when I say that heating the greenhouse was easy, it should not be assumed that the wood fire took care of itself. Cutting, chopping, and stacking firewood is by no means an easy task, nor is getting up every three hours during the night to keep the fire fed. It was simply an easy choice because we

167

were making do with what we had and determined to make it work no matter what.

On a regular basis we would check all of the working parts of the long-wood furnace. We checked the body of it, we cleaned the ashes, and we kept the area in front of the stove clear of debris and fire hazards. When you heat with wood, as we always have, it becomes second nature to ensure that everything is safe around the stove.

I don't remember exactly what I was doing on that cool spring evening when my pleasant farm dream came to a rather harsh end, but I do recall the fear that filled me when my nephew Ben came running into the DeMille farmhouse yelling "Vernie! The greenhouse is on fire!" It didn't register at first, It always seems that surprising events take some time to assimilate, but as soon as I understood what he was saying, I raced out of the door screaming "William!" Over and over and over again. My first thought was fear. What if he were in the fire? How bad was it?

It was bad. As I raced out of the door the flames were already completely engulfing the shed that housed the long-wood and the pile of wood beside it. They had jumped up to the poly-vinyl greenhouse film that covered the frame of the house and thick billows of choking black smoke filled the sky.

I never had a conscious thought of "I think I will risk my life to save my husband." I don't think I had time to consider all of the consequences of my actions. I simply ran right for the flames. I called for William; I got as close as I could to the shed, but there was no sign of him. I prayed as I ran to the other end of the greenhouse "Please! Please! Let him be okay, let me find him!" I ran into the house, the covering was on fire and dripping onto the ground, little fiery droplets of molten plastic hitting the garden beds. William was nowhere to be seen.

I have experienced true terror only a few times. That was the first.

From behind me, outside of the greenhouse I heard Ben shout again "He's here! He's here!" I ran back out and saw William coming across the lawn toward me, safe, and whole, totally unharmed. I cannot express the relief I felt. It was all encompassing. I ran to him and held on for just a few seconds while the inferno raged and then we got to work.

William ran to a pile of straw bales that the flames were licking at and tore it down so that it wouldn't catch. A propane tank stood on the other side of the burning furnace shed and he raced around to try and clear any flammable materials away from it. My brother and several of his children raced with us, trying desperately to move any fuel away from the flames, but it burned so hot and so fast that it engulfed everything around it within minutes. I went back into the smoke and flame choked greenhouse and started pulling out anything that would burn or add to the fire. I couldn't get it all, the flames moved too fast. They jumped to the small propagation hut and it burned to the ground in less than five minutes.

The greenhouse itself took longer. We finally just stepped back and watched. The polyvinyl burned then gutted itself out, then lit again and dripped to the ground as the fire continued to belch out the black smoke that we later learned was visible from 30 miles away. We stood there on the green lawn. I recall it was my favorite time of day, the gloaming, when everything is green and violet and golden. It was total devastation, months of work destroyed, but William with his usual humor turned to my brother's wife Joy and said, "Hey, do you have any hot dogs or marshmallows? We're got ourselves a pretty good fire here." We all laughed; what else can you do when your dream is raining down in plastic puddles?

The local volunteer fire department showed up and put out the last of the blaze. Our neighbors came by to mourn, laugh, and work with us. There wasn't much to do after all was said and done, just check all the smoldering piles to make sure no hot spots remained. It was over in less than

an hour. Months of work, prayers, hopes, and dreams were gone.

I will forever admire my husband for his courage in this situation and many others like it. You can't farm, or live for that matter, without tragedy and destruction striking from time to time. He waded into a situation that was frightening, with no certain outcome, you might say a losing battle, and did everything in his power to save what he could. He knew he couldn't save it all. He knew that any hope of an early crop that meant our success that year was already gone, but he never stopped trying. He never once said, "I don't think my effort will make any difference."

I lay in bed thinking of this story all morning. I honestly haven't thought of it in years, but it struck me in the early hours of the day that what he showed me that day was courage. He could have wept, he could have cursed. He could have shook his fist at God. He could have yelled "Why me?!" But he didn't. He could have stayed safely on the sidelines, waiting for the local fire department to arrive and cursed them later for being too slow. He could have assumed that it was someone else's responsibility to fight the fire he saw destroying that which he loved. But he didn't.

> I believe that courage is a direct result of love, and love is something that grows with action and use. Love doesn't just happen; love is cultivated just like a garden crop.

How often do we wade into a fire to save what or whom we love? How often do we have the courage to rush into a future we can't see and risk getting burned because there are some things worth fighting for; because there are some things worth risking our own comfort for? It's easy to stand on the green grass and watch the world burn around us. It's easy to watch while others labor for our good.

Perhaps I'm just too much of a farmer to want to choose the easy path. Perhaps I have seen enough of what happens in our lives when we don't fight for what means the most to us. We have experienced many crop failures in our life together. If we were smarter, and certainly saner, we would probably give up farming altogether, but there is something in the soil that always pulls us back. We picked up the pieces of that burnt out greenhouse, we raked up the debris and tilled the earth again. And when we plunged our hands back into that rich, black midwestern soil, we found something that we thought we'd lost: comfort. Because, you see, comfort wasn't to be found on the green grass doing nothing; comfort wasn't to be found in standing around waiting to be saved. Comfort was in the labor for something that will last well beyond our own lives. Comfort was in knowing we had the courage to race into a losing battle and fight for something that was precious to us.

There is so much of fear in the world right now. There is so much uncertainty. We have friends and family whose lives are falling apart, who have lost jobs, homes, careers, marriages, and the list goes on and on. How do we go on? The answer is simple. It is profound, and it is hard. The answer is: Courage. And how does one gain courage? I believe that courage is a direct result of love, and love is something that grows with action and use. Love doesn't just happen; love is cultivated just like a garden crop. It is a result of tending, continually weeding out of selfishness, and nourishment and thought for the future good of the garden itself. That which we love has the power to move us to action. That which we serve builds love in our hearts.

Comfort, courage, and crop failures; they are inseparable. This is the Law of the Harvest. You reap what you sow. If we live our lives in fear, comfort eludes us for at the end of the day it isn't the measure of our ease that satisfies us, but the measure of our heart and dedication. Find your courage today and fight your battles, push back at fear and you will find that you have pushed forward towards your own goals and dreams.

The Color of Abundance

Principle #19: Rejoice in today, it is everything we have

I was on a field trip with my son during the fall last year, walking through the forest around Wood's Lake in the San Juan Mountains, when it struck me suddenly what autumn smells like.

It smells like purple.

There are so many scents to autumn; it's hard for most people to narrow their favorite down to just one. Just a week ago I was picking out scented candles and the store had a few selections that were supposed to be reminiscent of the fall of the year. They offered "mulled cider," "pumpkin pie," "apple spice," "mandarin cranberry," "toasty fireside," and a few others. They all smelled wonderful; in fact I bought a jar of each because who can decide on just one? But there wasn't a single scent that gathered all that autumn is for me and bottled it up to be taken out and enjoyed later.

But as I walked through those woods in late September I finally got the purple fragrance of fall. From the rich Murex snail shell stains of the Phoenicians to the cloaks of kings, and from pop icons to little girls' "princess power" playthings, the color of purple has been well loved and used in human history. It was the foundation for an entire civilization, the color of segregation in South Africa, the color of new life to the Roman empresses in the Porphyry, the color that separated the kings from the commoners, and to me the color of abundance.

Abundance is at the heart of autumn. My husband William often comments on the wealth of late summer and autumn in the garden. The summer fruits are still growing, the winter crops are finally maturing, the gathering in of crops begins and there is plenty and to spare on the farm table. It is every gardener's delight.

It is also every gardener's sorrow. For with the arrival of the harvest abundance comes the awareness that the winter is ahead. The garden will become lean again, the soil that sustains us will grow cold and still, and the splendor of the leaves in their finery will give way within days to the bare beauty of limb and vine. While we gather our crops in the warm afternoon sunshine, placing the hubbard and banana squash in the root cellar, the apples in the basement, and the cabbages beside them, we are already fretting over whether

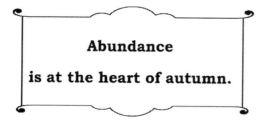

Abundance

is at the heart of autumn.

we have enough wood for our winter fires, enough blankets on the beds to keep out the chill, and as parents whether or not the children will need new coats and caps this year. Even in the midst of all the bounty, the subtle bite in the wind reminds us to prepare for what is coming in the months ahead.

It seems to be the season of reminders. It pushes us to remember what has been and to rejoice in it; to look forward to what will be and to prepare for it. It is absolutely the season for teaching us to live in the present—to look around at each breathtaking moment and soak it in. The gentle stroke of the wind sent showers of aspen leaves skittering across my path as I watched the children that day in the San Juan Mountains running and laughing through the forest, the leaves fluttering around their feet, twirling with the least provocation into a frenzied dance. The youths gathered them up by the armfuls, flinging them into the air just to watch them fall again. The death of the year was all around

them and yet they rejoiced, without fear, in the beauty of the Earth, accepted, without qualification, the gift of life today. Indeed, I have a suspicion that when the snow is falling, instead of the leaves, they will be equally filled with joy at the gift.

And so I walked through that landscape, relishing the moment, embracing life in the midst of the dying leaves and breathed deeply of all that the world around me had to offer. This is what I breathed that day: the crisp smell of fir and spruce needles, the clean smell of a mountain lake, the pungent odor of decaying aspen and oak leaves, the dry smell of finished pumpkin vines, and the sweet fragrance of apples fallen from the trees.

This is the smell and color of Abundance; this is the smell of purple.

The Humility of Planting

Principle #20: Grow in faith

The planting of any kind of seed requires a certain amount of faith in something beyond what we can see, hear, or touch. It is the very essence of humility. By planting a seed we take our hopes and dreams, our fondest desires and lay them in the ground with nothing but faith that they will rise again from that clay and blossom into fruition. We subject our will to that of providence, the elements, and the capricious whims of the earth. There are no guarantees in gardening; there are no certainties or promises. The soil doesn't come to us begging to be used. The trees and vines will not chastise us if they are not planted along our fields. Nothing pulls us to a garden but our own humility.

It is one of the first lessons of the Georgic tradition. The earth could get along without us. The fields would grow thick with grass and vegetation of many kinds. Animals would fertilize it, worms would till it, and rain would water it. It is we who are the beggars—we who come time and again with our meager offerings of hoe and rake and seed, and beg of the land and her creator a harvest.

We sow our seeds in humility and with faith we wait for the true leaves to appear.

The Blessing of Perseverance

Principle #21: Tend the earth for future generations, persevere in goodness that they might reap peace

Have you ever really watched a flower grow? Have you seen the first leaves spring from the soil and reach up to the sun? I confess I never have. It always seems to happen when my back is turned.

While I was busy one morning, hanging laundry on the line, my lilacs were opening up to full bloom. I didn't watch it happen but the fragrance washed over me while I was occupied with my work, and in that small instance I was surprised by joy. That is the blessing of perseverance. We do not plant our seeds, prune our roses, and weed our beds just so that we can then sit back, twiddle our thumbs and fret over when the harvest will arrive.

True perseverance is jumping up and getting to work.

True perseverance is jumping up and getting to work. It is doing the hundred other things that out of necessity must fill our days. It is sowing the seed and going on with the work that must be done. It is pushing past worry with work and finding in little moments the treasure of joy.

How delightful it is to be surprised by the blossoms of a flower you have lovingly tended and left to grow as you have trained it. Perseverance is patience, not apathy; faith, not forgetfulness; work, not worry. Longfellow said it best, we must "learn to labor and to wait."

The reward of a garden is not instant. It takes many years to see the harvest from a peach sapling and yet we plant anyway. We prune and train the young branches of a tree from which we may never harvest any fruit. It is perseverance that drives us on; the indomitable belief that we sow not only for ourselves but for our children and for the whole Earth.

The Glory of Labor

Principle #22: There is strength in laboring for what you need and for what you can give

We live in a time of confusion. It could be argued that there are many kinds of confusion and a multitude of papers could be written for them all. I will deal with only one.

Our society worships the human body. Billions of dollars are spent adorning it; concourses of people wear as little as possible with the intent of showing it off, millions are spent on implements of torture designed specifically for shaping it. And yet, for all our worship of the muscles and form of the human body, we despise the very element meant to sculpt it: we despise labor.

What we do not have to work for we value too cheaply. That which we labor for is too dear to be neglected.

It is an unwritten tenet of our cultural beliefs that something is sweeter if we can get it for nothing. Work that requires physical labor is low. I'm very much afraid that there are no John Henrys left in America to stand up and challenge the Iron Horse. No one left to question whether faster is better. If "manpower" no longer has any meaning, what is to become of man?

181

The human body is a thing of beauty and it was fashioned for physical labor. Not labor just for show, after all what good is image without substance? But labor for something greater than oneself. The greatest satisfaction in life comes neither from self-serving activities nor from self-aggrandizing pursuits. Satisfaction comes not from "having" and "doing," but rather from "acting" and "being."

A man of action, who sees a need and fills it, a man of principle who is unwavering in his dedication to correctness, these are the results of labor. Those who adhere to the belief that it is glorious to get something for nothing will never "have" enough, because there is no value attached to those kinds of possessions. Value is directly related to labor. What we do not have to work for we value too cheaply. That which we labor for is too dear to be neglected. A man who believes there is "nothing to do" and demands to be entertained continually values his life, time, and talents too little.

Labor adds value to our lives; it is the glory of the human frame and mind to "act" in such a way as to "be" a man of honor, integrity, and principle.

Glory is not to be had in things. It cannot be bought with bank notes nor can it be influenced by fame. Glory is only to be had in being who God means for you to be and acting as He would have you act.

The Hope of Harvest

Principle #23: Grief is an integral part of life, the part which sweetens our joy, and softens our heart

For me, Georgic farming has always been as much about cultivating virtue in myself as it is about claiming a crop from our labors on the land. The thing about developing virtues is that that they are often strengthened while you are feeling your weakest and least able to grow. They often find fertile ground in a broken heart or a disappointed one. They take root and bind up our wounds just when we think we can't keep going.

In reading some of these love letters, you will have found that one of the virtues I've turned to again and again is hope. Hope is precious to me and has always been. It makes me think of a tender seedling or newly sprouted seed. It is so incredibly fragile and yet is the foundation of such great things: joy, love, peace, and determination. They all begin their journey with hope. I have tried to nurture hope in my heart all my life, long before I knew or understood what Georgic Farming was all about. I pray you will forgive me for choosing to share the story that follows here. All of these stories have been of a personal nature; this book is after all, at the very core of it, a letter of gratitude to my ancestors, my family, my God, the universe at large for giving me the chance to "be." But this story...this is more deeply personal than the others.

This love letter is for someone I never met but whom I will always treasure and love. I seldom grieve in public. I cry in public; I have tear ducts that are sympathetic and have their own sense of timing. They have been known to go off easily, but seldom from grief. I weep when I'm happy or when my heart is overwhelmed with gratitude. Grief is different, and I usually choose to grieve alone. I learned the power of shared grief from my best friend through this experience. I learned it from William.

William and I were married in the spring of 1995, both of us 21, deeply in love, and full of the wonder and excitement of starting our life together and the adventure of where it would take us. It's crazy now thinking back to those first years. I often say to William, "We were nuts!" We didn't know very many details of how we would reach our goal, but we knew what our goal was: farming. Both of us wanted more than anything to farm full time—to draw our living from the land, to pour our hearts back into it, and live our lives intricately woven into the ebb and flow of seasons, springs, and harvests. We wanted to share the beauty of it with our children and the simple wonder of watching, cultivating, and participating in the continuing creation that is farming.

We worked, laughed, labored, and loved it all through 2 years, 4 different homes, and 1 piece of farmland. But we were missing something. We wanted something that spoke of future harvests, of lasting legacies, and the embodiment of our joy in living. We wanted a child.

I had fully expected as a newlywed in 1995 to come home from the honeymoon and start counting down the days to getting a nursery ready. I wanted to welcome in the next New Year with a brand new baby. William and I loved the time we spent together as just a couple; but both of us had learned early on in our lives to treasure family, and we were anxious to start our own. The longer time passed the more anxious I was. So in the spring of 1997 when I found that I was expecting a baby, I was overjoyed. I started collecting buntings and tiny shoes, reading parenting books, and

184

crocheting a baby blanket. There was fertile ground in my heart where love for my child could grow. I held the knowledge that I was now a "mother" like a bouquet of beautiful flowers that everyone could see and rejoice in with me, and they did. Friends, family, and associates celebrated with me all the new baby things I found and my fun in learning about names. My joy knew no bounds it seemed in preparing hearth and home for a tiny new soul. Even morning sickness, which is a misnomer and should more accurately be called "all day" sickness, couldn't diminish my happiness.

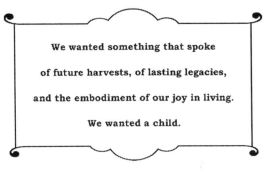

We wanted something that spoke of future harvests, of lasting legacies, and the embodiment of our joy in living. We wanted a child.

Everything was right in my world: a husband who loved me, friends and family nearby, a few acres to farm, and my own baby on the way. I was feathering my nest in anticipation, trying to take care of my body and the new baby's as best I could, and filling my mind with the knowledge I knew I would need when he or she arrived.

On a warm early summer evening I took my little, three-year-old niece Amileah to play at the park in town. We drove up and down the back country roads, singing silly songs and eating ice cream cones. I couldn't wait to have a little one of my own. "They'll grow up to be friends," I thought. "Her mom and I will be celebrating years from now when they welcome their own babies into the world." I curled up to sleep beside William that night, content, grateful, and happy.

I woke in pain. Not a rush of pain or even a sharp one; just a consistent and constant ache in my lower abdomen. I thought nothing of it at first. My digestive tract hadn't worked right for three months, and I just figured this was an extension of the discomfort of pregnancy.

As the morning progressed and my pain worsened I spoke to William about what was happening. He held me and comforted me, and when I looked in his eyes I could tell he knew. He knew before I did that the tiny life inside me was ending before it had a chance to hardly begin. I don't remember if I cried. I just remember thinking, "Keep it together, Vernie, just keep yourself together."

William drove me to his brother's house where we borrowed the phone to call my mom and my midwife. Sylvia, my sweet sister-in-law, put her arms around me and wept for me while I couldn't. I didn't dare let one tear go, not when I didn't know what was on the other side of them; not when I wasn't sure if I could stop.

My mom drove me to my midwife's office several hours away from our rural farm. I don't remember anything we said. I do remember stopping at my sister's house first and staring at a solitaire game on the computer screen. That's how I felt...solitary. Everyone wanted to comfort me, everyone wanted to ease my pain, and I didn't know how to let them. I laid on the exam table at the midwife's while she tried to find the heartbeat that had been there less than two weeks ago on my last visit, the soft, hummingbird speed "whoosh, whoosh, whoosh" that had filled the speakers. But there was nothing: just nothing but static as she moved the monitor across my belly.

That's how I felt inside—nothingness and static inside my heart.

As she finished her exam she told me "Well, you've definitely been pregnant. Your cervix is flattened. It only makes that shape after a pregnancy."

Had there been a concern that I wasn't "really" pregnant? Were people going to think that it was all pretend? Did this somehow not count? She gave me a handful of pills to take. She said they would help the contractions I was already feeling to do their job better and clean out my uterus.

"Yes," I thought bitterly. "Let's make sure to keep my empty womb tidy."

They worked. We were about an hour away when I asked my mom to pull over at a local Wal-Mart so that I could use the restroom. The pain and pressure in my abdomen was incredible.

I'm not sure I can adequately explain the horror that I went through in my mind inside that bathroom. My body was wracked with contractions, one after the other, again and again, while I sat in a filthy, cramped little bathroom stall with a broken lock and graffiti on the door. I wanted to scream, to weep, and tear my hair. I felt myself slipping nearer to the edge of hysteria as all hope of a reprieve from my own personal hell slowly bled out of me.

I could hear women enter and leave the restroom. When I knew I was alone, I let myself moan like some kind of downed, dying animal; when anyone walked in, I held my hands to my mouth so that no one could hear. I couldn't stand the thought of anyone else knowing of my pain, my grief, my absolute horror of finding myself giving birth to what would have been my baby in a cubicle designed to remove human waste. My baby was not waste! But what could I do? I wanted a soft bed and tender hands to hold me. I needed what I couldn't express and inexplicably felt ashamed of my need.

Finally the contractions eased, what had felt like an eternity was probably only a handful of minutes. I felt hollowed out and cold inside but there was such a need in me to maintain the appearance of calm. My mom drove me home, we stopped by and saw my Dad, and they both held onto me and told me how sorry they were. I knew they meant it, they grieved too. William held me when I got home. We talked, he held me, and I tried to function as best as I was able. I told my family and friends, "I figure I have two choices. I can feel sorry for myself or choose to be happy. I'd rather choose happiness."

I wanted to believe it. I wanted to believe that it was that easy, that if I went through the motions of happiness, it would be true. If I gave the appearance of strength, I would actually be strong. I tried to turn my back on the pain and heartbreak of the miscarriage, just taking it out to polish once in awhile like a trophy I could hold up and say, "Look what I went through, but see? I'm happy, I'm strong. Can you see how strong I am?"

William was a rock through all of it. I think he knew how much I was hurting. I don't think he knew how to get me to talk about it. He knew me better than I knew myself I think, and I in my own grief had failed to see his heart at all.

Then one day, about two months after my miscarriage I walked out of the farmhouse to go get William and bring him in for dinner. I saw him standing in his garden, hoe in hand, his back to me, looking out over his field. It wasn't an uncommon thing for him to do; he often stands still and just looks over his fields. I'm not sure what propelled me over to him. I could have just hollered at him that dinner was ready, but I wanted to be by his side so I walked over as the sun was setting, bathing everything it touched in gold.

He wasn't looking at his fields.

He was standing in his garden, clutching his hoe like a lifeline as tears poured down his cheeks.

"William!" I cried, "What's wrong?"

He turned his beautiful drenched eyes to me and he said chokingly "I wanted our baby, Vernie. I wanted our baby. I'm so sorry we lost our baby."

It shocked me as nothing else could have and his need touched me in a way that all the sympathy in the world could not. I hadn't believed before then that he could understand, but he did. Better than anyone else in the world he could understand because it hadn't been just my baby I lost that day; it had been his baby too. And he had had no one to share

his pain. I had been trying so hard to be strong that I had forgotten to let my heart be soft.

His need for comfort touched me and we held on to each other in our summer garden, weeping for our lost child and sharing one another's grief and heartache. Our mingled tears melted the cold inside me that had formed in that tiny Wal-Mart bathroom. My own grief eased when I finally reached out of myself to help my husband, and it was never so deep again. There were hard moments over the next several months. I think the most difficult was when Sylvia gave birth to her fourth child and brought him home. My arms ached when I held him and gave him back to his mother.

Seasons move steadily forward on a farm whether you're prepared for them or not. Sometimes we are late getting our crops in or we plant early and winter decides it wasn't done. Fall nears its end and we harvest crops that would do better with more time on the vine but time isn't to be had. Sometimes we harvest in fear of a frost and autumn lasts for nearly six weeks longer. There are no guarantees in farming. We simply do our best in the time that we are given. We learn to read seasons and weather, what rain and frost smell like in the winds of a seemingly warm day, and make the best choices we can over our stewardship.

"Steward" the term was always been used to refer to the man who ensured there was food for the kings and their people. As our technology has increased it has been used to refer to those who ensure that when you travel by boat or plane you are taken care of and more recently it has become a popular word among those concerned with our environment and the ever increasing impact civilization has upon it. But in all of these professions and movements it denotes the same thing: a willingness to care for, labor for, and be responsible for the home, property, life, and goods of someone else. Modern farming has become less and less about good stewardship and more about profit and loss, political lobbying, and ledgers. I was watching interviews from an agri-business trade show several years ago when the leader of a large, well-

known seed company said with pride "We're not farmers, we're businessmen." All I could do was raise my eyebrows and say "Amen. Thanks for finally confessing."

It's not that farmers are not businessmen, truthfully they have to be good businessmen. It is part of their stewardship, their responsibility to the land, the land which they view as not inherently theirs but rather something they hold in trust for their children, grandchildren, and so on.

A farmer, a good farmer who understands stewardship, will make choices for his land, animals, and family that may mean a smaller margin of profit but a healthier pasture. He'll make choices that mean a lower rate of field production but greater nutritional value in the crop. A good steward isn't looking to increase tractor speed so that he can get rid of another employee or sacrifice a harvest in ten years by applying chemicals today that will yield results but leave him dependent upon the fertilizer company because he killed all of the microbes in his soil.

Good stewards are always looking for ways to balance efficiency and husbandry, to find a way to be a good caretaker of both land and family. Sacrifices have to be made by both from time to time. It's the natural way of things. Rivers flow and land is sacrificed in the process. Winter snows come to fill the mountains with moisture and crops die from the cold. A sick but beloved animal has to be put down, when all treatments and medicines have failed, in order to preserve the rest of the herd. A favorite climbing tree has to be cut down when it's no longer safe to play on. Sometimes the planned family outing has to be canceled because a cow is calving or a ewe is lambing. That's what stewardship is about. It's about having a clear enough view of your goal as a farm family to withstand the struggle of seasons, weather, finances, life, death, and grief.

William taught me that grief is an integral part of stewardship as we held onto each other in the golden-tipped gloaming of our Missouri farm field. Sometimes we do our

best, we try our hardest, we struggle towards our goal, our harvest...but we don't make it. We run out of time, resources, and strength. But it's all a part of what stewardship entails. It's learning from mistakes, finding a better path, learning a new method, or traveling a new way. It's taking everything you've learned; everything you've felt, both joy and sorrow and moving forward with your ideal firmly fixed in your mind.

We didn't stop wanting a family at our first failure. We made the grief of loss a part of ourselves, and as William told me when we held our first-born son in our arms a year later, "We're better parents today than we would have been a year ago. We wanted him more because we understand better what loss is."

It was the hope of a future harvest that kept us going when it all seemed pointless. It is the same hope that drives us on each new season. It propels us forward to meet new friends, to learn better methods, to rejoice in harvests to share, knowing full well that if we fail, that if by some chance it doesn't work out there will still be more seasons to come and new opportunities with each one.

Thirteen years have passed since I opened my heart to grief and found comfort, 13 years of seasons that have brought change, joy, sorrow, peace, poverty and prosperity. Hope is still alight in my heart as I near this year's harvest, as autumn slowly gains a stronghold in the air and in the fields. And most evenings find me walking across gilded blades of grass, through glittering motes in the hay barn to William's side; and when he holds my hand and smiles at me, I know that it is thanks to him and to the strong but tiny souls that we have loved together that my heart is lighter, fuller, and stronger than it was before. And I can't help but feel when we stand together bathed in the gold of sunset, surrounded by lowing cattle and scratching turkeys and chickens, that I am the richest woman in the world.

The Love of Family

Principle #24: We all belong to one another

It would seem that the title of this love letter is self-explanatory and universal. It's generally expected that most people love their families, either the one they come from or the one they create or are welcomed or adopted into. It's a fundamental, foundational belief across generations, cultures, languages, religions, political parties, and creeds...love your family. I think I've been very obvious throughout this work so far about how I feel towards my own family and the intensity of the love I have for them.

The idea of familial affection speaks to the best that is within us because, let's be perfectly honest, sometimes it is a struggle to love your closest relatives. It's nearly impossible to live near and have a relationship with your parents and siblings, in-laws and cousins, grandmas and grandpas without friction developing from time to time. Tempers can flare over something as inconsequential as dirty socks or as seemingly insurmountable as adultery. Those who love one another deeply can jump to choose sides, misconstrue motivations, misinterpret words, judge harshly, or withhold affection, support, and any outward sign of kindness in an attempt to remain uninvolved in personal differences of opinion and perceived slights.

It can be a rough road to travel at times, especially since we all drag along our collective baggage with us. And sometimes when one member of the family finally lets go of

his own baggage, there are others who, not as ready to let it go, feel compelled to go through that dirty laundry and stuff it in with their own bags and bring it along on family vacations, to reunions, and on cross-country road trips.

As family members we can support one another better, defend longer, wound deeper, and disappoint more than anyone else on Earth. No one else's studied disregard or casual indifference can hurt so deeply, and no other gentle hug and whispered, "Good job!" means so much. We are often privy to the best and worst in each other and are by turns both less and more forgiving than the rest of the world as well.

We may love or loathe one another; we may distrust or admire or envy or pity one another because so many emotions are tied up with family relationships, but at the core of it is one basic idea; we belong to one another. "Warts and all," as my mother says.

This belonging requires a conscious effort on the part of all family members to look well beyond their own comfort, their own well-being, and their own satisfaction to seek out the needs of each other and help to fill them. I don't know how old I was when this notion really took a hold of me, but I'm guessing it was sometime around the summer I turned eight. Up until then I had derived great pleasure in being the evil tormentor of two of my older brothers, Aaron and Jared.

We would sit in the back seat of our old green Cadillac as it cruised down the narrow two lane highways, Aaron and Jared by the windows, me in the middle, and I would worm my hand down by their legs and pinch them. There was a reason for pinching their legs and not their arms; Mom and Dad couldn't see me do it. My brothers, not being as sly and devious as I was, would respond with a good honest punch on my arm, which mom and dad could see. I would proceed to bawl and carry on with a wonderful dramatic flair after which mom and dad would launch into the "Don't hit your sister" talk. I'd smirk or stick out my tongue at my brothers, and

they'd frown and silently threaten to pulverize me later. I never felt sorry about this until my eighth summer when I did it for the last time to Jared. I pinched, he punched, mom and dad lectured, and Jared gave me such a look of utter distaste for my behavior that I actually felt bad. I was shocked. The punch was nothing, that was just a couple of kids playing around, but that look? It really knocked me for a loop and my mind started working.

It made him feel bad when I teased him? He felt bad when we played nice one minute and I was mean the next? It was hard to shed my little narcissistic cocoon; it was painful to find myself experiencing emotions outside of myself. It would be nice to say that I never went back to teasing my brothers, but remember I was eight and it was a relatively habitual behavior. But I gradually learned not to as I began to understand remorse and empathy the older I got. Although I should clarify that I only felt guilty for pinching Jared, Aaron liked to flip my ears and I figured he deserved it. Actually he still flips my ears by way of greeting, but since we live about 2,500 miles apart it has now become more nostalgic than annoying.

I understood sympathy as it related to my own pain. I didn't want to make Jared feel bad because then I'd feel bad. It was still a kind of self-serving niceness, an avoidance of pain rather than a conscious seeking to do good in spite of it. I spent the better part of my teenage years trying to understand that principle better, the wanting to perform good works out of a sincere desire. Sometimes I got it right, more often than not I didn't. The blessing of a family is that you get the opportunity to keep trying. Each new day you have the opportunity to try again to serve with love, to develop compassion, and to better understand mercy.

Becoming a mother in 1998 intensified my feeling of selfless love. The first time I held my eldest son in my arms I began to realign my thinking, the way all mothers must, into recognizing that he wasn't "me" anymore. Not my body, as he had been, not just an extension of myself as I thought of him

at first. He was Ezekiel; he was unique, himself, totally new and undiscovered. I couldn't wait to hear his thoughts and know his feelings; and I was certain as I held onto him that I would do anything I could to protect him. It was a strange and terrifying emotion to love that deeply and recognize in the same instant that it was my job to raise him in such a way as to ensure that he could survive without me.

When I found myself pregnant with my second child I was worried. I honestly couldn't comprehend loving another child as much as I loved Ezekiel; he was just such a wonderful little boy. How could anyone else come close to touching that depth of love I felt for him? I didn't think my heart had room for any more love and I worried about whether I could be a good mother to both of them.

But then Ephraim was born and it was as if my heart had grown inside me just as surely as he had. When I held his tiny little body to my breast, stroked his cheek as soft as a butterfly's wing, and felt his little fingers hold tightly to mine, I could feel it swelling into new life, beating stronger than it had before. I hadn't realized until then that there was more love to be had, that it is not a finite commodity. With the birth of Ephraim I found more love for Ezekiel and William as well, more love and gratitude for my parents and grandparents, more appreciation for my brothers and sisters, and a greater tenderness towards other children that were not mine.

Zeke was three and Eph was one in the late summer of 2001, and life was exciting. William had worked for Doc Windom for over five years as a veterinary assistant. He loved the work, loved working alongside Doc, who was a wealth of knowledge when it came to animals and the progress of agriculture in the Midwest over the past 40 years. William learned so much more than husbandry on those trips with Doc. He learned the impact of subsidies on farm families, the real cost of CRP and he saw firsthand the gradual dismantling of the greatness that was mid-America. A desire was born in William as he and Doc drove those once thriving back roads, a desire to teach people what farming used to be about, that it

was more than profit and loss statements, more than insurance claims and government handouts. He wanted to show people that it has the capacity to be the foundation, the role it has always played, in a civilization. He read, studied, and listened, and the more he learned, the more determined he was to be a voice for what farming could be, what we've always felt it should be.

He decided that summer to attend Northwest Missouri State University. It was only 50 miles away; he would learn everything he could in their agricultural education department and then he would teach. Little did we know then that it was not the answer he was looking for, that the education system was not geared to support and sustain independent land-owners or teach them relevant information.

> Love.
>
> When I held his tiny little body to my breast, stroked his cheek as soft as a butterfly's wing, and felt his little fingers hold tightly to mine, I could feel it swelling into new life, beating stronger than it had before. I hadn't realized until then that there was more love to be had, that it is not a finite commodity.

We hadn't heard of Joel Salatin then. We didn't know anything about groups like Local Harvest. We didn't know any of this yet and so we made plans to attend. We looked for housing in Maryville, and William still worked with Doc, treasuring the last few months he had to learn from him.

It was a beautiful Indian summer day in northwest Missouri that September when I drove William into town to Doc and his wife Joan's office. Doc did the vet work, and Joan took care of the books and customers. I drove over to my Mom's house with Ezekiel and Ephraim to visit. We sat at her kitchen table while the early morning sun filtered in through white Battenberg lace curtains and cobalt blue glass figurines and talked about my sister-in-law Joy's harvest party coming up in October. The boys were playing with building blocks in Grandma's play room; it was a simple, pleasant morning.

Then Aaron called. He knew Mom and Dad didn't have cable or satellite TV, so he said, "Mom, you need to turn on your radio. A plane just flew into the World Trade Center." She handed me the phone and raced over to her kitchen counter to flip on the old radio. Every network was talking about it.

I asked Aaron to repeat again what was happening and he said, "They don't know who it was but someone flew a plane into the World Trade Center in New York." My mind couldn't wrap around it. I think I asked, "On purpose? It wasn't just some horrible, freak accident?"

"No," he scoffed grimly, "It wasn't an accident."

"How did they get an empty plane into New York airspace, right into the city like that?" I asked.

"It wasn't empty. They hijacked it."

I think I handed the phone back to mom then. Not empty? I shuddered. How many people? I wondered. How many survivors? We didn't know about the second plane yet, we didn't know about the collapse of the towers. All I could think of was the plane.

William finished work early that day; I told him what I knew while I drove him up to his parents' farm, eight miles from our little house in Denver, Missouri. We watched videos on the TV of New York City. We saw the planes hit the towers again and again and again and again. Each time it was like a new wound. We saw the towers collapse and the gray dust and rubble cloud cover the city streets. As videos from amateur photographers emerged, we watched the same horror with new eyes.

William drove himself to work the next day while I sat, safe and warm on my couch, watching the war zone that New York had become. I watched as images of the Pentagon emerged, as a field in Pennsylvania appeared with a giant

black scar on the farm fields marking where flight 93 had crashed.

And again all I could think of were the planes.

I imagined myself on those planes. The networks showed pictures of the passengers and I wondered what would I have done if I had been one of them? If my child was sitting beside me and I knew we were flying to our death, what would I say? How would I comfort my child?

And suddenly, as I sat there contemplating the unimaginable and the terribly real, I was seized by an emotion I had never really felt before...hate. I had never known before that moment what it was to really hate another human being.

I hated, with an almost perfect passion, the men who had calmly looked into the eyes of their fellow passengers and then willingly murdered them. The hate was so huge it burgeoned up inside me like a bomb. It made my skin sensitive to touch, my ears attuned to more sound, and my heart cold. It wasn't enough that their bodies were disintegrated in the fire and buried beneath thousands of pounds of concrete and rebar. I wanted them to suffer more than death; I wanted them to know a greater torment. Hell was not even enough for me. I wanted them to be cast down past even the burn of the fires of brimstone to where they could rot in the cold and empty silence of nothingness, where they could exist in nothing but the horror of their own barbarism, cruelty, and damnation.

For hours and hours I could feel nothing but that all consuming hatred. I fed my children, I changed diapers, I started dinner, but I couldn't move my heart past the cold of my emotions. Finally I sat, with my children spread at my feet, watching it again and again and again. I don't think I realized I was weeping until Ezekiel put his little hands on my face and said, "Mommy, why are you crying?" I told him, as simply as I could that some very bad men had flown some planes into the

buildings and that I was crying because so many people had died.

"Why did they do it Mommy?" he asked.

I had no answer for him and none for myself so I just pulled him to me and hugged him until he squirmed away to go play with his blocks. His tender, baby boy hug calmed the hate inside, but I could still feel it threatening to overcome me. It drove me to my knees, and I pleaded with God to take it away, to remove the hate from my heart.

I believe in God. I believe in His active participation in my life. There have been too many miracles and moments of transcendent beauty and strength in my life to deny Him. This was one of them.

As I knelt there on the floor of my living room, my two sons playing beside me, pleading with the God of the universe to take the hate from my heart, I felt something shift inside my soul. I have discovered over a lifetime of praying, seeking, listening, and receiving answers that God doesn't just take things away. He replaces with something else. He doesn't exist in or create vacuums and voids in our lives. He replaces, fills, compensates, and redeems.

I didn't know it but that is what I was pleading for: redemption. And it came, as surely as sunrise and seasons, and was as painful as birth. Because in removing the hate from my heart, He replaced it with something else. Something I had felt twice before, only now it was deeper, richer, and more encompassing than I thought possible. It was painful to grow and to accept what He wanted to give me—to accept a parent's love.

At once, unbidden and clear the images of those planes filled my mind only now they were sharper and a terrible love filled me with joy and an aching sorrow. In the clarity of that moment a thought, both beautiful and agonizing entered my heart. It spoke to my mind words that changed me forever. "All of the people on that plane were my

children. All are my sons and daughters. All have need of my love and mercy. Forgive, for your sake. How much more need of forgiveness have my children who wound their brothers and sisters willingly? Whom would you have me deny?"

All I could think in response was "None." Somewhere in the Middle East there was another mother kneeling in prayer, seeking comfort in her loss; in England, New York, Japan, Australia, California, Mexico, Brazil, Kenya, China, and all over the world mothers were seeking comfort and peace in a world overrun with enough hate to fill an ocean. I couldn't bear to add one more drop. There were already enough hearts given over to the cold nothingness of hate, revenge, and terror. I didn't need to be another one.

Love, compassion, sorrow, and forgiveness swamped me. I trembled with the intensity and pulled myself up to the couch where I wept out my broken and newly bandaged heart. Ephraim crawled over and I picked him up to rock and feed him. Ezekiel climbed next to me and patted me on the shoulder.

I wept and wondered at the easy love between my sons, two brothers who had been friends all their short lives. From his first view of him in the hospital bassinet Ezekiel had cried out "It's Ephy!" as if he had just been waiting for his best friend to arrive. I thought of the troubled relationships of adult siblings, marred by anxiety, loneliness, resentment, and envy. I thought of parents who, no matter how old or young, worried over their children and choices they knew would lead to unhappiness and heartbreak, knowing every child must make their own decisions regardless.

My definition of family changed that day, and I was no longer just the youngest of twelve, or the last of the big parade. I was a daughter of the divine, a sister to the noble, a mother of heroes. I was also the daughter of transgression, the sister of fear, the mother of want and need. I was no more and no less than one part of a tremendous whole, and I had a role to play on this stage of my existence.

I had to choose.

In the end that was the answer to my prayer. God forced nothing upon me, because He never does. He simply allowed me to see the two paths before me and let me choose. Anger, hate, and a frozen heart or love, forgiveness, and a broken heart. There was no easy choice, there never is, but there was, for me, a correct one. I chose to love my family.

All of them.

Not just the ones that think like me, or look like me, or believe all the same things. I had been well taught after all, by my own parents, that we are a family because we choose to be.

Every day we live we are given the opportunity again to love our brothers and our sisters, to look past perceived differences to what makes us the same in our hearts. We all hope for a better world for our children, we all search for love and comfort, we all strive to find meaning in our day to day labors. Each new day we are again shown our two paths— love and life or hate and death. We walk in the paths our parents have shown us. We forge new ones that lead us to greater understanding and peace. We seek to know our legacy and either live up to or overcome it. We do the work required to ensure that our name is synonymous with generosity of spirit. We choose our place; and when we have chosen, we reach out to our neighbors, to those we come in contact with to build our family, our community, our world.

There is a need in the world for family. There is enough and to spare of violence, bitterness, and condemnation. It can be hard to stand in an angry mob and be a voice of courtesy, charity, and conviction. Hard because it is difficult for some to understand that peace is not passivity and that humility is not weakness. It is hard for some to understand that standing up for your personal truth does not equal a lack of consideration for theirs. It takes many voices to make a choir, each member singing their own part. An orchestra is richer for its diversity of sound—the melody, harmony, major, and minor notes all blending into a magnificent work of art.

The God that filled my heart with mercy on a beautiful late summer day in the middle of America made a world full of differences—mountains and valleys, deserts and seas, farmlands and forests. Opposites and opposition exist in the world, and all we can do is choose for ourselves.

> Every day we live
> we are given the opportunity again
> to love our brothers and our sisters,
> to look past perceived differences
> to what makes us the same in our hearts.

I look at my brothers and my sisters, some that share no common blood with me, and I see only hearts that love as I love and hands that labor to do good. The differences are lost in the depth of feeling we share with one another. We draw no lines in the sand that separate us. We have our differences and disputes but we draw a circle of love that welcomes everyone in to the warmth of family.

I look around me at the people I do not know, at the family I haven't met yet, and I feel the yearning to draw them in, to know them better, to welcome them home to my heart so they will know they are loved, they will know that they belong. Because in the end we all belong to one another. Warts and all.

Putting Down Roots

Principle #25: The greatest harvest of our labors is our own hearts, our own homes, and the strength of the communities we build.

It's mid-morning on a clear and cool October day. We've harvested vegetables and herbs from our fields to be sent to members of our farm. The cows have been milked and moved to fresh pasture, the pigs fed, and the chickens and rabbits in their "pasture schooner" and "bunny-mobiles," our movable livestock pens, transferred to new green grass. I'm only halfway through this week's laundry, behind because there is more work to be done in a day on a farm than we can possibly get to. My children are either working to clean the toy-strewn stairs or they have escaped to the barnyard where they are building a fort complete with water-filled moat. It's suspiciously quiet so I suspect the latter. I have a few quiet moments to myself as the rinse cycle finishes, and I am here in the house, looking out at the fields, pondering.

I spoke to my Dad just a few days ago and asked him about planting apple trees. He's planted more than a few in his life, and I wanted to get his advice. "Plant in the fall," he said. "The fall?" I asked. "We always planted in the spring back in Missouri. Shouldn't we wait until then?" "No," he responded "you need the deep soaking rains so that the tender roots will spread out as quickly as they can. By next summer they'll have a good enough base to survive when the dry days come. They'll be able to survive it and send their

broad roots down in search of water and nutrients. Plant them in the fall."

I've been thinking about that advice—that and other advice I've received from him over the years. Always keep your gas tank above half. Spend less than you earn. If you don't have enough money to buy it today, wait until you've saved enough for it. Don't jump into a deal just because someone tells you "this is a one of a kind offer;" there are a million one of a kind deals out there so make your decision based on principle not persuasion. Don't jump to conclusions. Temper your generosity with wisdom. Forgive and keep going, but don't let yourself get beat up again and again. Being a family means you stand up for one another when you're in the right and stand up to each other when you're in the wrong. Love means you do have to say you're sorry and "I forgive you." "I love you," "excuse me" and "please." And don't ask if the dress makes you look fat. If you feel good in your own skin, you'll feel good about what you wear. It's been over a year and a half since we stood in the kitchen in the old adobe house in Paradox Valley and talked about gratitude, faith, and service. William and I told Dad about what we had learned about helping other people, expressing thanks for the opportunity to provide service, and pursuing our goals with good works as our focus. I told him, "You know, financially we're probably in the worst spot we've ever been at in our lives. But emotionally and spiritually I feel better than I ever have. I can look around me and I don't feel poverty stricken. All I can see are blessings. I can pray, and my prayers aren't to please rescue me from money issues, heartaches, and disappointments; they're prayers of gratitude for friends and family and fertile fields." Dad nodded his head and said, "I'm glad you've learned that at your age. It took me longer to understand it. Success isn't money; it's doing something to help someone else. It's using your gifts and talents to serve."

I've revisited those words often. The vision that William and I share, the desire to add something of value to the world and to give our children a legacy to build on, is sometimes clouded by self-doubt, fear, and tremendous

feelings of inadequacy. Does anyone ever feel qualified to be a parent or change the world? Does anyone ever wake up in the morning and think I can handle anything life throws my way today? More often than not, I wake in the morning to find myself humbled by the beauty of the world around me, intensely grateful for the opportunity to live my life in it and pursue my dreams surrounded by its bounty. I wake with the desire to be a gentler mom, a more understanding wife, a more dedicated friend.

My parents made it look so easy. I've asked my Mom what her secret was and she just tells me, "Oh, you kids made it easy to be good parents." It makes me laugh, because I know I was a pill. I heard, "Vernie, talk softly your voice carries," often enough to know that I was a loud child. I've got enough clutter in my house today to know I was not neat as a child. I know there must have been moments when my mother grew frustrated with all of us, when she grew disgusted with dirty dishes, dirty diapers, muddy shoes, and endless laundry. I'm guessing that as a farm wife she too fell behind on washing dirty clothes when there was work to be done in the fields. Did she wake and feel no doubts? I don't think so; I think that doubt is a common plague upon mankind. Doubt is the gene that makes us question and leads to knowledge, makes us fear and acts as the catalyst to courage, makes us despair and drives us on to hope.

Do we fail when we doubt? Or is doubt simply the reminder that we are in fact human, fallible, prone to weakness, and capable of error?

I ponder all of these things as I look out at green grass that continues to grow even as the days get shorter and the nights colder. I look across the grass to the evergreens and oak trees that mark its boundaries as they begin to drop the fruit of their summer labors: acorns and pinecones. I ponder on the inevitability of change and the things that are left behind.

Every autumn the beauty of the tree leaves increase even as their existence comes to an end. William, who is a scientist at heart, explained to me once that the color of the leaf is always there. We just can't see it because of all the chlorophyll present while the leaves are busy doing their job of photosynthesis. Is it an accident which has no merit in our lives that the leaves are most beautiful just before they fall to the earth to return the nutrients it took to produce them back to the soil, or that a flowering plant will produce more prolifically when it knows it is nearing the end of its cycle? Does it have any bearing on our decisions when we hear stories of the Chinook salmon, the fish that uses the last of its strength to return to its breeding grounds just to spawn and die? Do we stop to wonder at and yearn for the dedication of a bird like the penguin that will go for months on end in the bitter cold with no sustenance just to ensure the safety of first its egg and then its chick? Or do we see a lesson in the valiance of one honeybee who will expend all of her energy in working for the good of eggs and larvae that were not birthed by her? Everything in the natural world moves toward a harvest; every plant, animal, season and soil moves toward death, rebirth, and a continuing regeneration of itself. There is no planning beyond natural selection and instinct that propels it forward, but so it moves year after glorious year. It is only mankind that faces the decision with every successive generation: what will we give up that we may move on?

There is an old Greek proverb which states "A society grows great when its old men plant trees under whose shade they know they will never sit." I have walked beneath the bowers which my forbears planted. I have stood beneath cathedral trees and felt the love for them and what was learned in their midst, planted by the hands of my progenitors bloom in my heart. I have trod fields once bloodied by brothers slain and wept for the loss of freedom, liberty, peace, and life. I have walked storied halls of national history and seen the courage and sacrifice that has brought me to where I am.

There have been many "old men" in my family's heritage who have planted trees that I may be sheltered and shaded in my need. They have planted seeds of faith, love, and hope which have bloomed in the fertile soil of my soul. And now I watch as my own mother and father reach the apex of their growth, this season of autumn in their lives. I watch them with my children, see the love in their eyes and in the gentle touch of their hands upon their heads and can finally see, as their life's labors recede, the true beauty of the lives they've lived.

They have colored my days with love, generosity, faith, wisdom, and an unflinching dedication to following correct principles with exactness. As the harvest for which they have worked all their lives springs up around me and my brothers and sisters, the grandchildren, and great-grandchildren of our family, they ever so slowly and gently drop their blessings upon us. Little words of wisdom when we don't think we need counsel anymore, a call in the middle of the day when we didn't know anyone knew we needed a word of love, and a letter in the mail with an angelic smiley face to punctuate a grandmother's love all rain down upon us like the falling leaves of a spreading oak.

> "A society grows great when its old men plant trees under whose shade they know they will never sit."

I see them in their glory and I realize that I must make the same choice that they did so long ago—the decision that their parents made before them and theirs beforehand, and so on throughout time.

I must put down roots.

Every oak drops its acorns in hopes that new trees will grow, but in order for a new oak to grow the acorn must cease being an acorn. It must send roots deep into the earth and a

tender sapling up into the light of the sun. It must leave the safety of its mother's branches and fall into its father's fields.

How grateful I am, in the midst of my own "becoming" that I was given the chance at a tender age to see the vastness of the land in which I may grow.

I have yet to find my place, but it hasn't stopped me from putting down roots. Everywhere I have had the privilege to live there have been lives that have come into mine that have enriched my days. Like a companion plant that sustains while it is sustained they have brought me peace, joy, comfort, and experience while giving me the opportunity to serve and be served. Everywhere we have gone as a family I have had my own harvest, my children, near me to share in the wonder of all we learn and seek.

In the end it is for them that I search for my place. It is for them that I seek to know my strengths and weaknesses that I might pass on only that which will help and heal.

It is for my children that I plant apple trees in the fall. It is for the hope of their children's children's harvest that I seek for the strength to become what I know I can be and more than what I am. It is for the beauty of a world in which they can walk without fear, without bloodshed, in peace, and freedom that I labor.

I till the soil, I plant the seeds, and I tend the crops that my children may walk in truth through my father's fields.

Epilogue:

Finding Home

*Principle #26: To be an American is not to own a right, it is to
step up to a responsibility*

When I was born in San Jose, California many years
ago my parents gave me something that is precious to me;
something that spoke to them of their love for one another,
their family, and their love for me.

They gave me my name.

This name that I bear came to mean something to me
over the course of my young life. All the time I was growing
up I knew of no other little girls named for their fathers and I
delighted in the knowledge that I had been given a variation of
my dad's. I loved that whenever my family called me they
included my middle name (which I share with my mother) in
their hailing. Each time I was spoken to it was a vocal
reminder of their togetherness, their bond, and their
continuing commitment to their promises to each other.

When we embarked on our first road trip across the
country I had already received that first gift, given almost in
the instant I was born. I knew in large part what my name
meant both to myself and to my family. I was not as yet
concerned with what the name meant to anyone else, that
was peripheral knowledge for me, but it was paramount to me
that I knew what it meant and that my family did too.

I was a Johnson. Unwritten in that title, but not unsaid, was an understanding that we stood for one another, we defended one another, we were loyal and we were loving to one another. I knew at seven years old, when we pulled out of Burney, California in that borrowed Winnebago who I was and where I came from.

That was my parents' second gift to me: I knew my roots. I knew that my family had a legacy. I didn't know it because I'd seen Wisconsin yet or Carbon County, Utah. I knew the foundation of my family because of the relationships nurtured with my grandparents, my brothers and my sisters. I knew that the principles of faith, love, and hard work were fundamental to my progenitors. I knew, without anyone having to sit down and explain it to me that I came from people who endured hard times because they believed with absolute certainty that better times were just around the corner. I felt the joy of tradition as we gathered together for holidays and birthdays.

> As we traversed back roads and cityscapes, trees and titanic columns of steel, mile by mile, and state by state my parents gave me a homeland.
>
> They gave me America.

I felt the celebration as I was included in rejoicing over new additions to our family through birth, marriage, and adoption. I knew this legacy and it was neither a crutch nor a burden, it was simply our story.

I loved to hear my parents and grandparents tell of my ancestors. Little Ethel, Uncle Arthur and his Duesenberg, Great-Grandma Britton with her sassy spirit, Benjamin Johnson and his barefoot faith, Julia Hills with her pioneer dedication, and dozens of other stories. They were more than just words on a page or bedtime tales to me. They were pieces of a chain reaching back through generations and I was just one of the newest links. With every family event held and every new family member cherished those links grew stronger

and firmer until they formed something it took me years to appreciate: an anchor.

As we headed out across golden hills, sage and silver deserts, grass green byways, and mirrored-blue waters I knew who I was and whom I came from. I was secure in myself, more secure than I was less than 10 years later as a young teenager, and I was sure of my family. I never doubted that they were mine or that I was theirs. I knew that they would hold onto me.

As we drove slowly up Colorado mountain passes made navigable by past generations and crossed rivers with ease on well-built Mississippi bridges, as I stood at the feet of heroes carved on a South Dakota mountainside and walked reverently down a worn forest path in New York state I came to grasp what my parents were giving to me. I reached out and took it with both hands, savored and remembered it. But I'm not sure I fully understood what I had been given until I sat down to pen these letters and to give the feelings of my heart words and freedom.

As we traversed back roads and cityscapes, trees and titanic columns of steel, mile by mile, and state by state my parents gave me a homeland.

They gave me America.

As we stopped to visit places I had only read about in books or heard about in stories the reality of my legacy came alive. I saw the ruts in the rocks where wagon wheels had sliced their way through the earth. I saw a modern mix of concrete and grass where an entire generation had gathered to stand with a man who refused to be oppressed, who spoke out and gave his people courage, who continued to dream and whose dream still lived on. I felt the power of it and the dream became mine.

I walked into the capitol building where men and women debated, argued, blended, and mixed their ideas to best represent the people who had sent them there to govern.

I listened as a proposed change to water rights in California, a subject that as a farmer's daughter I was very familiar with, made its way around the room. I sat in the cafeteria at the capitol, eating an enormous piece of Lemon Meringue Pie, while senators and representatives from all sides of the political spectrum discussed over lunch a way to meet the needs of so many different people. I rode in the elevator with Tip O'Neill, then speaker of the House of Representatives, and the distance between a little California farm girl and "the powers that be" in Washington D.C. diminished. I saw those men and women laboring for what they believed in, laboring for what I believed in and realization dawned that I was one of the "we" in "We the people".

We watched as "Old Glory" was displayed behind a special glass case while the national anthem played. We stood just inches away from the documents that had severed forever our governmental tie to Mother England and established a nation of our own.

I knew my ancestors had fought in the war for our independence, that they had defended what had become their homeland with their lives, property, and honor. It meant more to me as I saw the banner and read the words that had given them hope and freedom.

I wondered at the kind of love so powerful that it would drive a man to give up comfort to fight for freedom. I wondered at a faith so deep that it would be enough to strengthen the wife who let him go and took up the reigns to tend to that which he fought for. I wondered at a hope so bright that the children of those brave patriots could look forward with absolute certainty to building a nation founded on principles of liberty, equality, providence, and self-reliance.

It kindled a fire in my heart to feel the echoes of their sacrifice and the determination of their spirits in that place dedicated to preserving, defining, and defending that which makes us American.

Place. That is the gift my parents gave me that summer, had given me at Hillcrest Orchards, and continue to give me with their current farm in the heartland of America. It is a gift to know your place in the world, to know it and to love it. Not with a love that is blind to its problems, or oblivious to its beauties, but with a love that sees what it has come from, what it is, and what it can be in the future if enough care is taken with its course.

I loved Hillcrest Orchards not because it was perfect, I pulled enough weeds to know that it wasn't, but because in spite of its imperfections it produced something beautiful, sweet, and nourishing every year at harvest.

I love America for the same reasons. I've seen enough of her to know that there are weeds that need pulling, fields that need tending, entire systems that need to shape up and pull their own weight. I have also seen her beauty, her compassion, and her determination in the face of terror, discouragement, and despondency. I have seen her greatness in the faces of her people. In the hands of those who serve and the hearts of those who reach out in love to understand a neighbor, a stranger, and even an enemy.

A place, a name, and a legacy: three things which are vital to our continued success as individuals, families, communities, and as a nation.

Do we know who we are? De we know or care what our name means to those around us? Our name should be synonymous with the principles that we espouse and we should safeguard the names of others in our homes. I can't help but believe that our civilization would improve if we were all more "civil" in how we speak to and of each other.

Do we know from whom we come? Do we know our legacy? There are many children born today with no fathers and often no mothers, who spend their youth passed from foster home to foster home. I have friends who provide several of these brief havens for children who are refugees of

a war being waged in homes against drug and alcohol abuse, physical, emotional, and sexual abuse, and the apathy of parents so mired in poverty they can't see the treasure they have in their children. Do these children exist without a legacy simply because of when, where, or how they were born? I don't believe so. I believe it is the imperative of every person born to this earth to live up to or to overcome what has come before him, and for most of us it is a little of both. I hope that my children will not inherit my faults or my fears. I hope that they make better choices that lead them to greater happiness.

I hope that every child growing up in America today will know that he has the potential for greatness inside him. I hope that every child growing up in America today knows that she has the power to change the course of the future simply by making good choices. I hope that the children of America today will choose to live and leave a legacy of dedication to the same principles that gave us our foundation.

Do we know our place? Do we know what it means to be American? De we know, understand, and love our homeland? I have stood under the parched and baking heat of an Arizona sun and watched my mother give water, food, and compassion to a man who was ragged, worn, and weary because he believed in the promise of America enough to risk his life to find her. I've watched with horror as those who call themselves "Americans" have thrown stones at the hungry, tired, and wretched of the earth because their skin is the wrong color, their accent is unacceptable, and their assumed motivations misunderstood. I watched, cried, and understood then that this glorious place we call America is not just a birthright to be hoarded jealously, it is an idea worthy of sharing. Not with force; so that it chokes and suffocates those with whom we hope to share liberty with, but with open-handed, honest fairness that enables all who wish to partake of it to accept at their own pace and to integrate the power of freedom into their own homeland, their own legacy, and empower them to love and appreciate the grandeur of their own name and place.

To be an "American" is not to own a right, it is to step up to a responsibility.

To be an "American" is to give with gratitude, receive with honor, trade with integrity, build with care, and dream with determination. We must never let our plenty lead us to believe that we are better, nor our poverty to discourage us into believing that we are less. In order to be "Americans" we must accept both our greatness and our ghettos, our nobility and our need. We must not rob one to feed the other, but rather lift all within our borders to a new height of knowledge, productivity, dedication, and ultimately happiness.

> **3 Things**
>
> A place, a name, and a legacy: three things which are vital to our continued success as individuals, families, communities, and as a nation.

It will require the same strength of will and character that led a handful of men and women to forge a new nation. It will require the same compassion that welcomed those who were considered the refuse of other lands and turned them into the backbone of a great society. It will demand the same pride that could proclaim a Scottish, Armenian, Ukrainian, Brazilian, or Chinese heritage without sneering at another in contempt for theirs. And above all it will ask for our love. A deep, profound, and motivating love for each other as we are and for whom we can be. Love allows us to set aside fear, prejudice, anger, and hurt. It is what will move us forward as a people. "Love one another" isn't just a good idea or a noble ideal. It is our only hope.

I have one request as I pen this last love letter and share a hope that has been ridiculed and rejected in the past for being too simple, too naïve, and ineffective at changing the world. Take out a piece of paper, find a pen, and write a love

letter of your own. Write it for your parents, for your spouse, for a friend or for your children. Tell them your story, who you are, where you've come from, and where you hope to go. Your story matters.

Make your name mean something great, live up to your potential, find your homeland and leave a legacy behind you that will inspire the greatest generation that will ever live to build a civilization that will never fail.

Made in the USA
Charleston, SC
23 August 2015